SINGER

SEWING REFERENCE LIBRARY

Clothing Care & Repair

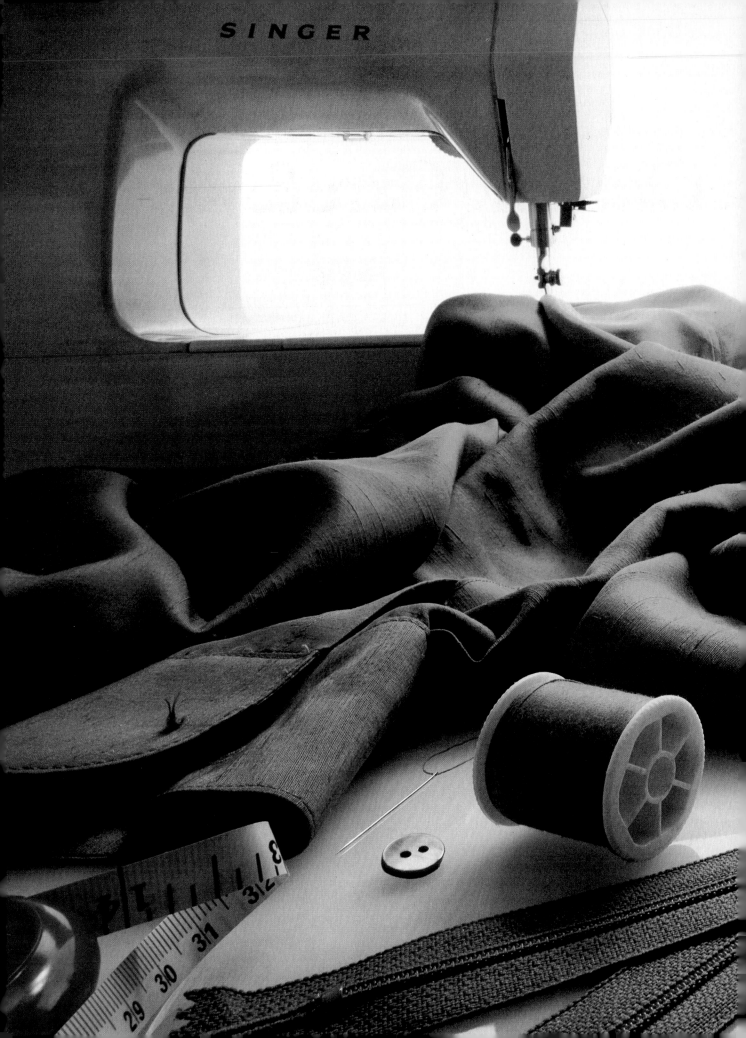

SINGER

SEWING REFERENCE LIBRARY

Clothing Care & Repair

Contents

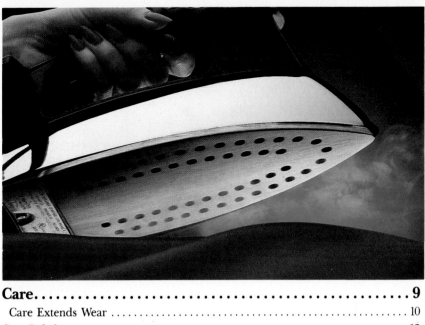

Copyright © 1985
Cy DeCosse Incorporated
5900 Green Oak Drive
Minnetonka, Minnesota 55343
All rights reserved

Library of Congress Cataloging in
Publication Date
Clothing Care & Repair.

(Singer Sewing Reference Library)
Includes index.
1. Clothing and dress — Care. 2. Clothing
and dress — Repairing. I. Series.
TX340.C56 1985 646'.6 84-45776
ISBN 0-394-54490-0
ISBN 0-394-73417-3 (pbk.)

CY DECOSSE INCORPORATED
Chairman: Cy DeCosse
President: James B. Maus
Executive Vice President: William B. Jones

CLOTHING CARE AND REPAIR
Created by: The Editors of Cy DeCosse
  Incorporated, in cooperation with the
  Singer Education Department. *Singer* is a
  trademark of The Singer Company and is
  used under license.

Project Director: Gail Devens
Project Manager: Bernice Maehren
Art Directors: Susan Schultz, William Nelson
Editors: Paula Brewbaker, Reneé Dignan, Susan Meyers
Writers: Lavern Bell, Janet Hethorn, Elisabeth Jones, Susan Meyers, Lois Millner, Jeanne Olive
Sample Supervisor: Phyllis Galbraith
Sewing Staff: Bridget Haugh, Carol Neumann, Marie Castle

Director of Photography: Buck Holzemer
Photographers: Tony Kubat, Jerry Robb, Martha Sherwood
Production Director: Christine Watkins
Production Manager: James Bindas
Production Staff: Michelle Alexander, Julie Churchill, Christopher Lentz, Douglas Meyers, Nancy Nardone, Jennie Smith, Nik Wogstad
Consultants: Lavern Bell; Pat Dorff; Rubye Erickson; Wendy Fedie; Janet Hethorn,

Lois Millner; Zoe Graul, The Singer Company; Chris Mason, Jim Nelson, HomeStyles
Contributing Manufacturers: Closet Maid by Clairson; Elfa® Storage Systems; Basic Line Products; The Singer Company; Risdon Corporation; Suzy Sewell, Handweaving Originals
Color Separations: La Cromolito
Printing: R. R. Donnelley & Sons Co.

SINGER
SEWING REFERENCE LIBRARY

Clothing Care & Repair

How to Use This Book

Your wardrobe is an investment contributing to your image, so you expect the clothes in it to look good, to feel comfortable and to last. To stay in good condition, a wardrobe requires a simple, efficient routine of care that includes periodic repairs and updating.

Clothing Care & Repair presents easy, proven techniques for clothing maintenance, and it serves as a source of practical ideas for repairing and updating clothing. It's a book for everyone, from the young person looking for the basics of long-term wardrobe upkeep to the experienced homemaker with an established routine of clothing care. To use the information in this book, you do not have to know how to sew; you do not even have to own a sewing machine.

The book contains facts, charts and procedures you may often need, so it is arranged to be used as a reference, as well as a source of ideas. It is divided into three major sections: *Care*, *Repair* and *Customizing*. Each section provides you with a general overview followed by specific tips and techniques. Close-up photos are accompanied by step-by-step instructions to guide you through each procedure.

To be useful, the three sections do not have to be read in sequence; each contains independent techniques and instructions. But when the book is read as a unit, it presents a complete plan for wardrobe upkeep and management.

Care

Care is everyday maintenance. To help you with your overall maintenance plan, this section contains a guide to fibers and finishes, and an explanation of terms used by clothing manufacturers on their permanent care labels. With these guides you can judge, before purchasing, which garments and fabrics fit into your clothing care routine.

A major part of that routine is keeping clothes clean. The laundry procedures presented in this section are uncomplicated but updated to include procedures for cleaning new man-made fibers. Because removing a spot or stain may mean the difference between discarding a favorite item and continuing to enjoy it, a spot and stain removal guide is included for reference.

The clothing care process also includes clothing management: organizing closets for family members, storing seasonal garments and packing clothes for travel. Modern products, such as vented storage containers, plastic-coated closet hardware and tubular hangers, can save time and space. Whether you are reorganizing your closet or planning a trip, you'll find practical ideas in this section to make the job easier.

Repair

In the *Repair* section the emphasis is on choices of techniques. We have included easy non-sewing methods, as well as techniques for hand or machine sewing. Choose from numerous methods for making common repairs, such as sewing on buttons, applying patches, and repairing hems or zippers.

With modern products and procedures, clothing repair is no longer the time-consuming chore it used to be. Sewing machines now have increased capabilities. You can also simplify repair techniques by using time-saving conveniences, such as fusible mending aids, fabric glue and portable mending appliances. Yet quality is not sacrificed; these products result in a sturdy repair, often less visible than one done by a more traditional method. Use the technique that works best for your specific need.

Customizing

Routine clothing care and repair can keep your wardrobe in good, serviceable condition, but customizing can extend the life of your clothes even further. Customizing can improve the fit of a garment or update its fashion details. The change may be as simple as raising the hem of a dress or as major as redesigning the collar and lapels of a jacket. Our sewing consultants have included ideas for customizing that are most often in demand or that result in an attractive new style without requiring extensive sewing expertise.

Our goal in giving instructions for altering the length or width of a garment is to help you personalize the fit of your clothes. If the garment fits well, it is more comfortable and attractive, and you'll wear it more often.

Customizing may also call for updating the style of a garment. By updating an article of clothing you can achieve a completely new look without remaking the whole garment. You'll learn how easy it is to make a skirt from a dress or to completely redesign a neckline.

Clothing care, repair and customizing need not involve a lot of time and money. You can personalize the ideas in this book to make the most of your own resources. Whether you have a great deal of sewing experience, or none at all, turn to *Clothing Care & Repair* for practical choices in wardrobe care. Use it to help you extend the life of your clothes.

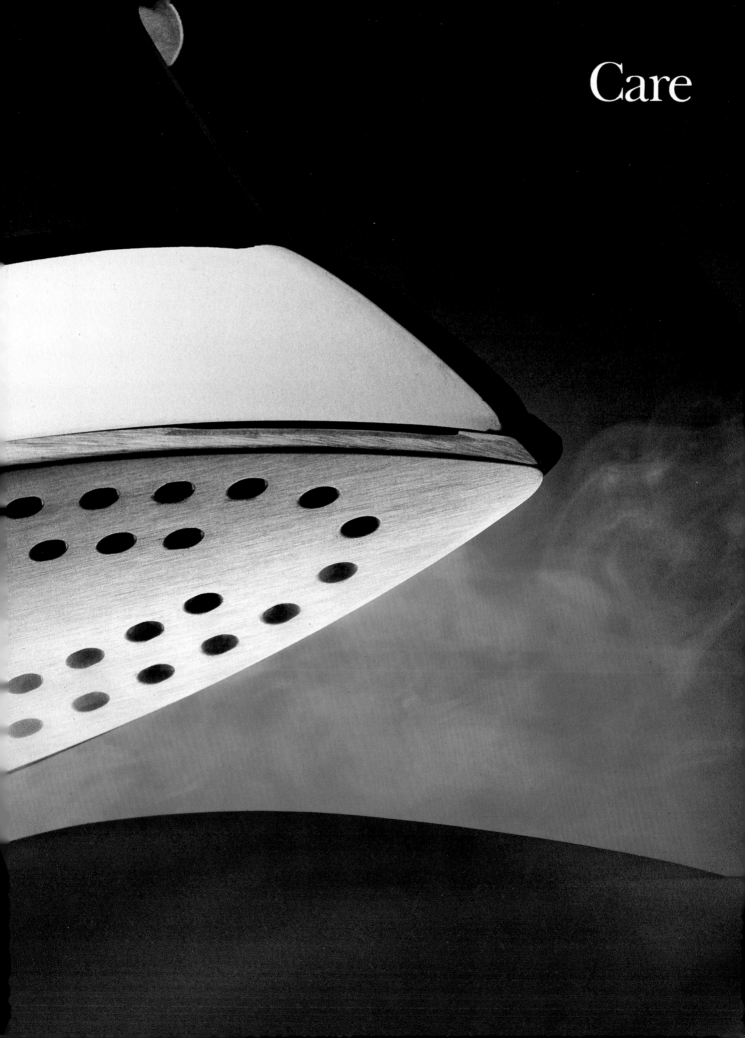

Care

Care Extends Wear

Care of your clothing may be a behind-the-scenes effort, but the results are clearly visible in your everyday appearance. Day-to-day maintenance keeps your clothes fresh, clean and comfortable.

Awareness, more than skill, is the key to developing a routine for clothing care that includes airing, brushing, ironing or pressing, cleaning, and removing spots and stains promptly.

When you purchase a garment, the ongoing process of care begins. Before you buy an article of clothing, decide how much time and effort you are willing to put into its care. If you know, for example, that you have little time to spend on clothing care, you may decide against buying a white linen dress that will require frequent cleaning and pressing.

Garment hang tags and labels spell out specific clothing care requirements determined by the fiber, fabric, finish, trimming and use of the garment. Polyester/cotton clothes have become popular because of their easy-care characteristics — machine washable and dryable with little or no ironing necessary. Fabrics such as silk and velvet, white and light colors, and garments trimmed with metallic and beaded trimmings are high-maintenance items which require extra care or special handling.

Before a purchase, examine the quality of the garment's fabric and construction. The hand, or feel, of the fabric should match the reputation of its fiber. Good quality corduroy is soft, not stiff; linen is crisp, not limp; terrycloth is thick, not sparse. The more you comparison shop, the more familiar you will become with the quality of fabrics.

Woven fabric should get its firmness from threads per inch, not sizing added to give temporary body. Once fabric with temporary sizing is washed, it becomes limp and the garment may not hang well. To check for sizing, grasp a section of the garment in each hand and rub the two surfaces together to determine whether sizing flakes off and leaves the fabric limp.

Details that Determine Quality

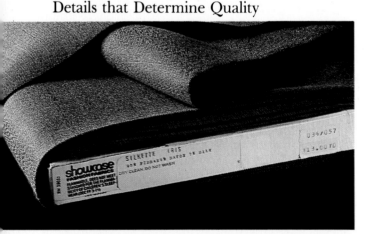

Care and fiber information is on fabric bolts.

Hems are even; seams have finished edges.

10   **Plaids** match.

Check seams for smoothness, uniformity, and finished edges. Be sure that all stitching is strong, unpuckered and reinforced at stress points. Hems should be even and invisible. Topstitching should be straight and unbroken. Finally, look for careful detailing, such as plaids that match, zippers that are durable and hidden, buttons that are sewn securely in place, collar points that match, darts that lie flat.

Avoid future repairs by checking the overall fit before buying. Poor fit leads to broken zippers, split seams and worn fabric.

Keep a simple record of clothing purchases as an aid in wardrobe planning and upkeep. File hang tags, extra buttons and matching threads or yarns in a card file. Save the hang tags because they often have more complete information than the sewn-in label. A little time spent in filing these items can be well worth the effort when you need the button, thread or specific information from the hang tag.

A clothing care routine extends the wear of your wardrobe and saves you time by preventing problems. Clothing care means more than regularly washing or cleaning your clothes. It entails a long-term plan for day-to-day maintenance, including an organized closet and storage for out-of-season clothes or garments that may be saved and passed on to a younger family member. How carefully you store your clothes affects how often and how much care is needed.

Clothing cleaning processes that you need to be familiar with are machine washing and drying, hand washing, drycleaning, and stain and spot removal. Reading and understanding care labels is a simple approach to determining which process to use. Special instructions for stains are not usually included on care labels, but a knowledge of fibers and fabrics will help you know how to remove difficult stains. For these, use the stain removal guide in this section as a reference.

Topstitching is straight and unbroken.

Collar points match.

File hang tags, extra buttons and thread from purchased garments.

Trims are securely attached.

Hang tags spell out clothing care.

55% SILK
20% ACRYLIC
15% ANGORA
10% NYLON
RN 62616

DRY CLEAN OR HAND
WASH WITH CARE
IN LUKEWARM
WATER, RESHAPE LAY
FLAT TO DRY.

Care Labels

Today's fashion garments combine a wide array of fibers, constructions and finishes. The federal Care Labeling Rule, revised in 1984, requires clothing manufacturers and importers to attach *permanent care labels* to their products. Labels can help you make purchase decisions based on clothing care requirements. They also help you avoid damage to your clothing from improper care.

The Care Labeling Rule also applies to fabrics by the yard. Care and fiber information is located at the end of the fabric bolt or roll. Record these care instructions and add them to your card file of hang tags and garment notions.

To eliminate extra work and expense, check the bolt-end labels before buying fabric. Simplify future care by selecting garment components, such as buttons, trimmings and interfacings, with the same care requirements. If the fabric is washable but the buttons are not, you add the cost of drycleaning or the time of removing the buttons before washing, to the cost of caring for the garment.

Labels also serve as an implied warranty. If the garment is damaged during cleaning or laundering when you have followed the prescribed care instructions, return it to the retailer or the manufacturer. If you need information about the manufacturer that the retailer is unable to give you, look for the manufacturer's RN or WPL identification numbers on the garment label. With these numbers, you can trace the name and address of the manufacturer through your local library.

Care Label Terms

Washing

Hand Wash	Use gentle hand squeezing action for fabrics unable to withstand machine agitation. Rinse well. When no temperature is given, hot water up to 150°F (66°C) may be used.
Machine Wash	Adjust machine water temperature and length of cycle to prescribed setting (WARM or COLD, below). When no temperature is given, hot water up to 150°F (66°C) may be used.
Warm	Use water that is hand comfortable, 90° to 110°F (32° to 43°C). Warm water removes soil from heavily soiled items better than cold water.
Cold	Use water as it comes from tap, up to 85°F (29°C).
Do Not Have Commercially Laundered	Use home or self-service laundry only. Fabric or garment cannot withstand high temperatures or strong cleaning solutions used for industrial or institutional laundry.
Small Load	Wash with a smaller than normal load to reduce overcrowding and allow garments to tumble freely.
Delicate Cycle or Gentle Cycle	Use slower agitation and reduced washing time for delicate fabrics such as lingerie, sheers and laces.
Durable Press or Permanent Press	Use cool rinse before spinning to avoid setting wrinkles in fabric when machine washing.
Separately	Wash garment by itself because of its bulk, tendency to bleed, or tendency to shed or attract lint.
With Like Colors	Wash with colors of similar hue and intensity to prevent bright colors from bleeding onto lighter-colored garments.
Wash Inside Out	Turn garment inside out to protect right side of garment.
Warm Rinse	Use warm water, 90° to 110°F (32° to 43°C), to remove soap residue from hard water.
Cold Rinse	Use to prevent heat-set wrinkling. Cold rinse, up to 85°F (29°C), can usually be used to save energy.
Rinse Thoroughly	Rinse several times to remove detergent, soap and bleach.
No Spin or Do Not Spin	Remove garments at start of final spin cycle to avoid wrinkling or twisting out of shape, especially for drip-dry or knit fabrics.
No Wring or Do Not Wring	To keep from twisting out of shape or setting wrinkles, do not wring by hand or with roller wringer.
Damp Wipe Only	Wipe with damp cloth or sponge to clean the surface of fabrics that cannot withstand dipping in water.

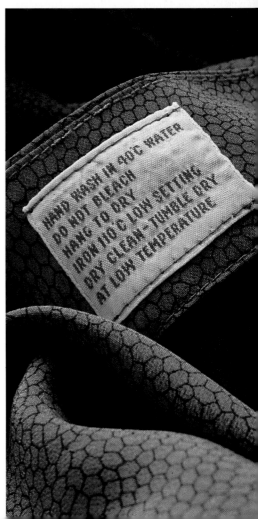

Bleaching

Bleach When Needed	Add chlorine or oxygen bleach as needed to wash cycle to whiten, disinfect and remove stains from fabrics.
No Bleach or Do Not Bleach	Fabrics that are non-colorfast or have a flame-retardant finish cannot withstand bleaches which may weaken fabric, cause colors to bleed, or turn whites yellow or gray.
Only Non-Chlorine Bleach When Needed	Use only oxygen or non-chlorine bleaches to whiten or brighten. Use only when necessary. Fabric may be damaged with use of other types of bleach.

Drying

Tumble Dry	Use machine dryer. When no temperature setting is given, a hot setting may be used. To allow items to tumble freely, do not overload dryer. Do not overdry.
Medium Heat	Use MEDIUM HEAT (on some dryers, this is the PERMANENT PRESS setting) to prevent wrinkles or damage by high heat.
Low Heat	Set dryer at LOW HEAT to prevent fabric damage, shrinking and set-in wrinkles.
Durable Press or Permanent Press	Set dryer at PERMANENT PRESS setting for most synthetics and blends. Cool-down cycle reduces wrinkling.
No Heat	Set dryer to operate without heat to remove moisture from heat-sensitive items.
Remove Promptly	Remove dry items from dryer at once to prevent wrinkling.
Drip Dry	Hang dripping wet garment on rust-proof hanger. Hand shape and smooth if necessary.
Line Dry	Hang damp items from indoor or outdoor clothesline. This label is often used for fabrics that would shrink or stretch out of shape in a dryer.
Line Dry in Shade	Hang these items on a clothesline out of the sun to prevent fading or sun damage to fabric.
Line Dry Away from Heat	Dry items away from any source of heat to prevent shrinkage or hard, stiff finish.
Dry Flat	Lay garment horizontally for drying to maintain its shape.
Block to Dry	Reshape garments by hand to original dimensions. Dry flat.
Smooth by Hand	While garment is wet, smooth to remove wrinkles, straighten seams and flatten puckers.

Ironing & Pressing

Iron	Fabric requires ironing. If no temperature is given, HIGH temperature setting (COTTON, LINEN, WOOL) may be used.
Warm Iron	Use MEDIUM temperature setting (RAYON, POLYESTER, SILKS, BLENDS) for fabrics that cannot tolerate high heat.
Cool Iron	Use LOW setting (ACETATES, ACRYLICS, SHEER SYNTHETICS) for fabrics that cannot withstand medium temperature.
Do Not Iron	Garments with this label are made of fabric that could melt or lose a textured finish if ironed.
Iron Wrong Side Out	Turn garment inside out to protect the right side of fabric, such as nylon, dark cottons and corduroys.
Steam Press or Steam Iron	Use steam setting on iron at appropriate temperature for fabric. Moisture can be safely used on fabric.
No Steam or Do Not Steam	Do not use steam on fabrics that could shrink or be damaged by excessive moisture. Metallic fibers can tarnish from steam heat. Crepe may shrink from steam pressing; taffeta and satin may lose luster.
Steam Only	Steam without touching iron to fabric to prevent flattening the surface of fabric. This label is often used on napped or pile fabrics, such as corduroy or velvet.
Iron Damp	Sprinkle or dampen fabric, usually cotton or linen, before ironing to aid in removing wrinkles.
Use Press Cloth	To prevent iron shine or scorching, place damp or dry cloth on top of fabric before ironing or pressing.

Drycleaning

Dryclean
Clean with a solvent, using any commercial process that may include liquid, hot tumble drying, and steam pressing or finishing. Bulk or coin-operated cleaners may be used.

Professionally Dryclean
Use full-service drycleaner for optimum results, requesting modifications specified on care label. Do not use bulk or coin-operated cleaning, which cannot be modified.

Petroleum, Fluorocarbon or Perchlorethylene
These solvents are used to dryclean garments and to remove stains that are not water-soluble. Drycleaner should use the solvent(s) specified.

Short Cycle
Drycleaner should reduce cleaning time for delicate fabrics, or for the specific solvent used.

Minimum Extraction
Professional drycleaner should use least possible extraction (spin cycle) time.

Reduced Moisture or Low Moisture
Drycleaner should decrease humidity for fabrics that may shrink with normal drycleaning moisture.

No Tumble or Do Not Tumble
Drycleaner should not tumble-dry fabrics that are loosely woven because of possibility of thread slippage.

Tumble Warm/ Tumble Cool
Drycleaner should tumble dry at specified setting for heat sensitive garments that would melt or lose luster.

Cabinet Dry Warm/Cabinet Dry Cool
Cabinet drying at warm or room temperature is done by professional drycleaners for fabrics that cannot be steamed.

Steam Only
Do not press or iron the garment when steaming. Fabrics with nap or pile are crushed by pressing.

No Steam or Do Not Steam
Do not use steam in pressing, finishing, steam cabinets or wands.

Leather Clean
Take garment to a professional drycleaner who uses special leather or suede care methods. With other methods, leather may dry out and stiffen, and colors may bleed.

Washing or Drycleaning

Wash or Dryclean, or Any Normal Method
Fabric can withstand machine washing in hot water, bleaching, machine drying and ironing at a high setting, or drycleaning with all commercially available solvents.

International Symbols

Washing symbol gives washing instructions: 60°C (140°F) means you may safely wash in hot water; 30°C (86°F) indicates special care is necessary.

Drying symbol indicates the garment may be tumble dried.

Triangle instructions pertain to chlorine bleaching.

Iron gives ironing instructions: one dot indicates cool iron; two dots tell you to use a medium iron; three dots mean you may safely use a hot iron.

Circle gives drycleaning instructions: A indicates all normal drycleaning methods; P specifies perchlorethylene cleaning; F indicates the "Solvent F" process.

X through symbol means DO NOT wash, tumble dry, bleach, iron or dryclean.

From Fiber to Fabric

The fabric your clothing is made from begins with fibers: fibers are made into yarns, yarns into fabric and fabric into clothing. Fibers largely determine the care your clothing requires. Care is also affected by fabric construction, fabric finishes and garment assembly. All these characteristics determine the manufacturer's recommendations on care labels. Thus, garments of identical fibers may require different methods of care.

When shopping for clothes, look for the fiber content label. Fibers are listed on the label by their generic, or family name. In addition, brand names such as Dacron® (DuPont's trademark) may also be used.

Compare the fiber's properties and characteristics to the qualitites of the garment that are important to you. For example, if you are shopping for a lightweight jacket that will be strong and durable, a nylon jacket is a much better choice than a rayon one. Knowledge about different fibers is also helpful when buying clothing without a care label, such as some items of used clothing.

Fabrics are made of natural fibers, man-made fibers or a blend of fibers. A blend is a combination of fibers, resulting in a fabric that has the best characteristics of two or more fibers. Polyester/cotton is a common blend found in shirts, blouses and many sportswear items. This fabric has the breathability and comfort of cotton with the easy care of polyester. The percentage of each fiber in a blend helps to determine which fiber characteristics will dominate.

The chart on clothing fibers, opposite, defines fibers, their care, characteristics and uses. To serve as a guide for general care, it includes the most commonly used natural and man-made fibers. For specific garments and blends, rely on the garment's care label.

Finishes are applied to the fiber, yarn or fabric during production. They may be applied before or after weaving or knitting to change the appearance, the hand, and the performance of the fabric.

A finish may be permanent or temporary; special care may be needed to make the finish last longer. Follow care instructions carefully. Some finishes, such as water-repellency and sizing, are renewable in the home or by a professional drycleaner.

Guide to Clothing Fibers

Natural Fibers	Clothing Uses	Properties	General Care
Cotton	Light and mediumweight garments	Strong, comfortable, versatile, durable, absorbent, wrinkles in use, will shrink.	Most are machine washable, regular cycle, hot water; dry on regular cycle; use hot iron.
Linen	Blouses, dresses, summer suits	Natural luster, strong, durable, absorbent, cool, somewhat stiff, wrinkles easily.	Machine wash, regular cycle, warm or hot water; dry on regular cycle; use hot iron; drycleaning may be desired to retain color and shape.
Silk	Light and mediumweight garments, scarves	Natural luster, strong, absorbent, does not wrinkle easily, takes dyes well, resists mildew and moths, weakened by sun and perspiration.	Most need to be drycleaned; some may be hand washed; do not wring or twist.
Wool	Light, medium and heavyweight garments, outerwear	Strong, resilient, warm, absorbent, takes dyes well, shrinks, attracts moths, has insulating capacity.	Dryclean except when labeled "washable"; knits may be hand washed with mild soap; dry knits flat to avoid stretching.
Man-made Fibers			
Acetate	Light and mediumweight garments	Silk-like, lustrous appearance, drapes well, dries quickly.	Drycleaning preferred; use cool iron to prevent shine.
Acrylic	Knits, outerwear, pile fabrics	Soft, resembles wool, tends to pill, dries quickly; resists mildew, moths, chemicals and sunlight.	Hand or machine wash; dry on cool cycle; use warm iron, never hot, for touch-ups.
Modacrylic	Deep pile and fleece fabrics, children's sleepwear	Soft, resilient, dries quickly; resists wrinkles, chemicals and flame.	Dryclean pile garments; some may be machine washed, warm water; dry on cool cycle; use cool iron.
Nylon	Lingerie, dresses, hosiery, outerwear, sweaters	Exceptionally strong, elastic, abrasion resistant, resilient, low moisture absorption, retains shape.	Hand or machine wash; needs little or no ironing if removed from dryer immediately.
Polyester	Wash-and-wear clothing, often blended with other fibers	Strong, resistant to stretching and shrinking, crisp, resilient, sharp crease and pleat retention.	Hand or machine wash; needs little or no ironing if removed from dryer immediately.
Rayon	Dresses, light and mediumweight clothing	Soft, comfortable, weaker than most fabrics, absorbent, lacks resilience.	Hand or machine wash, gentle cycle, lukewarm water; use cool iron; may dryclean.
Spandex	Foundation garments, swimwear, ski pants and other sportswear	Strong, good stretch and recovery, lightweight, resists abrasion, not chlorine-resistant.	Hand or machine wash, lukewarm water; drip dry or machine dry on cool cycle.

Guide to Clothing Finishes

Antistatic	Chemical substances absorb moisture to reduce static electricity and keep clothing from clinging.	Permanent press	Chemical treatment or heat-set process adds resistance to wrinkles during wearing and washing. Creases and pleats can be set.
Antiseptic	Chemical agents inhibit bacterial growth to reduce perspiration damage and inhibit odors.	Preshrunk	Shrinkage is controlled but garment may shrink slightly.
Crease-resistant	Fabric is resistant to wrinkles, but is stiffer and less absorbent.	Sizing	Starch-like substance added to a fabric gives extra body or stiffness; it may also add extra strength or weight. Sizing may be temporary.
Flame-retardant or flame-resistant	Fabric resists ignition or retards burning. It is required by law for children's sleepwear and other items of clothing. No finish is *flame-proof*.	Water-repellent	Fabric is treated with silicones to cause it to resist water. Finish is not permanent, but may be reapplied.

Stains

Success or failure in treating fabric accidents is much the same as treating any type of accident — emergency first aid often makes the difference. Without quick action, stains may be impossible to remove because a chemical reaction between the spilled substance and the fiber actually bonds the stain to the fabric. Sunlight, heat and time trigger these chemical reactions. For successful stain removal, apply the following rules to the treatment of every stain. Consult the stain removal guide on the next four pages for techniques for specific stains.

Act quickly. Blot or wipe the spill. Do not rub. A quick, cool rinse with water or club soda helps remove most stains on washable fabrics. For nonwashable fabrics, sponge with water or club soda, wetting fabric as little as possible.

Check the care label for bleaching directions, and washing and drying temperatures.

Pretreat any spot or stain before laundering. Washing and hot water can set a stain.

Test chemical solutions, bleaches or solvents in a hidden area first to make sure they do not remove color or damage the fabric. Test on a seam, inside a pocket or on a scrap of fabric.

Use weakest solution first.

Rinse well, several times if necessary, to be sure that all traces of solution are removed.

Air dry between efforts to remove a stain. Use a hair dryer, turned to a cool setting, to speed drying. Avoid heat from a clothes dryer, sun or radiator. Do not iron or press.

Heat a solution before increasing the concentration. Warming increases the solution's effectiveness.

Work on damp fabric, except for waxy stains. Keep washable fabrics moist until you begin treatment.

Repeat the procedure if removal is not complete. Traces of a stain can create future problems. Rinse well between each removal effort.

Laundry & Stain Removal Staples

Because promptness is so important in removing stains successfully, keep a selection of stain removal staples on hand. Start with one of each of the following categories, then build your supply according to your needs. Use each product as directed on the package.

Use caution in storing and using stain removal agents, especially bleaches, solvents and strong chemicals. Keep them tightly capped, away from food and out of the reach of children. As a further safety precaution, use solvents in a well-ventilated area, never near an open flame or electrical outlet.

Absorbents are applied to fresh oil-based stains to absorb them. They partially remove the stain to make cleaning easier. Apply to stain, let stand for at least 15 minutes (longer for some stains), then brush or vacuum off. Cornmeal, talcum powder, chalk, fuller's earth and whiting are common absorbents.

Bleaches are used to bleach stains and kill mildew. Oxygen bleaches can be used on all fabrics. Use chlorine bleaches on washable, colorfast fabrics. Hydrogen peroxide is a mild bleach that, when diluted, can be used on silk and wool. Also use vinegar, lemon juice (from fresh lemons, not reconstituted) and ammonia (in some cases). Use color remover for extreme cases.

Detergents, alone or in combination with mild bleaches, are effective stain removers on washable fabrics. Mild dishwashing detergents and dishwasher compounds can also be used.

Prewash soil and stain removers (combination solvents) are effective on oil-based stains. They contain drycleaning solvents in combination with detergents, glycerin and water. Use on washable fabrics before laundering normally. There are also special soil and stain removers for use on permanent press fabrics.

Enzyme presoaks and bleaches are used for protein-based stains, such as grass and blood, on washable fabrics. Dissolve powders completely or they may leave small white spots on fabric. After soaking, rinse well. Liquid laundry detergents, containing enzymes are particularly effective in removing protein-based stains in washable fabrics.

Solvents, such as drycleaning fluids, amyl acetate, spot remover, rubbing alcohol, acetone, nail polish remover, and paint remover or stripper, are used on oily and combination stains. Never use them in combination with water or in the washing machine. Be sure they are completely removed before placing clothes in the dryer. Acetone dissolves some synthetic fabrics, so test first.

Soaps, such as laundry flakes, bars and liquids, are used on delicate fabrics. In very hard water, they may be difficult to remove if water softener is not used. Rinse thoroughly.

Miscellaneous products that may be used are oxalic acid, rust removers and glycerin.

Stain Removal Procedures

To remove a stain or spot from a garment, begin with emergency first aid. Then perform the pretreatment for the stain as described on the chart, below. If the stain remains after the pretreatment, follow the instructions for treating bleachable or nonbleachable fabric before laundering the garment.

Bleachable fabrics are white and colorfast cotton, linen, polyester, acrylic, nylon and permanent press.

Nonbleachable fabrics are non-colorfast items, silk, wool, mohair, spandex and flame-retardant finishes.

If you are not sure whether a fabric is bleachable, test it for colorfastness. Mix a solution of 1 T. (15 ml) chlorine bleach and ¼ c. (60 ml) water. Apply one drop to an inconspicuous area of the garment. Let stand for one minute, then blot. If there is no color change, the garment can be bleached safely.

When treating a stain, place layers of clean, absorbent material, such as white paper towels or fabric, under it. This prevents the stain or solution from transferring to another part of the garment. For most stains, work from the underside of the fabric, forcing the stain out of the fabric and not through it. Replace toweling as stain releases.

To prevent fading or weakening of fibers, avoid soaking any stain in a solution longer than necessary. Check the stain after a minimum amount of time, usually 30 minutes; change water or solution, if necessary. Soak time depends on the promptness of treatment, the chemical reaction of the stain with the fiber, and the strength of the treatment. Some stains disappear in a few minutes; others may take overnight soaking. Be patient. It may be necessary to repeat a procedure several times.

When more than one step is given on the guide below, start with the first one. Proceed through the steps until the stain is gone. *As a last resort for bleachable fabrics, treat with a mild chlorine solution.*

Terms to Know

Agitate solution into stain by rubbing gently between thumbs until solution penetrates the stain.

Feather the outer edge of an area dampened with a solvent by lightly brushing with a white cloth or paper towel. Work from the outside in toward the center to prevent a distinct solvent ring.

Flush by rinsing fabric from back side under a strong stream of tap water. This removes cleaning agents and stains.

Force a solution or water through the fabric by placing the stain over a plastic pail or bowl. Pour the solution through the stain from arm's length above. Protect surrounding area from splashes. An alternative is to squirt the solution from a squeeze bottle. Either method usually needs to be repeated.

Enzyme paste is made by applying powdered presoak and a small amount of water directly to the stain. Work into a stiff paste.

Enzyme presoak uses 2 to 3 T. (30 to 45 ml) powdered presoak to 1 gal. (3¾ l) *warm* water. Use *cold* water for blood and egg stains. Soak stains for a minimum of 30 minutes. Do not use with chlorine bleach, which deactivates the enzyme.

Prewash soil and stain remover or enzyme liquid laundry detergents should saturate the stain. Wait a few minutes, then wash with detergent, unless directions specify otherwise.

Mild chlorine solution is a mixture of 2 T. (30 ml) liquid chlorine bleach to 1 qt. (1 l) water. Never pour undiluted chlorine bleach directly on fabric.

Spot & Stain Removal

Stain	Pretreatment	Bleachables	Nonbleachables
Alcoholic drinks	Sponge with cool water. Soak at least 30 min. or overnight in cool water & detergent.	Soak in solution of 2 T. (30 ml) chlorine bleach to 1 qt. (1 l) water. If fruit colored, use drycleaning solvent. Rinse.	Sponge with cool water. For stubborn stains, force water through stain.
Antiperspirant buildup	Wet. Rub in detergent or prewash soil & stain remover. Rinse. Air dry.	Soak in solution of 1½ t. (8 ml) oxalic acid to 1 c. (¼ l) hot water for 1 hr. Rinse; repeat two more times. Rinse with solution of ½ c. (120 ml) vinegar to 1 gal. (3¾ l) water. Wash.	Moisten area with hydrogen peroxide or oxygen bleach *after testing fabric*. Let stand for at least 30 min. Rinse. To restore color, use equal parts ammonia & water. Rinse.
Beer	Blot. Rinse with cool water.	1) Apply solution of a few drops vinegar or lemon juice to 1 c. (¼ l) water. Agitate. Rinse. 2) Work in enzyme paste. Wash.	Same as for bleachables.
Blood: fresh	Sponge with cool water. Keep area moist if possible.	Soak in cool water for 30 min. Flush with cool tap water. Soak in solution of 3 T. (45 ml) ammonia to 1 gal. (3¾ l) cool water for 15 min. Rinse. Work in detergent. Wash.	Dry after sponging. Apply hydrogen peroxide. Rinse. Sponge any remaining stain with oxygen bleach solution. Rinse. Treat with weak enzyme presoak solution *after testing fabric*. Rinse.

Spot & Stain Removal

Stain	Pretreatment	Bleachables	Nonbleachables
Blood: dried or set-in	Soak in cool soapy water, changing water as stain releases. Rinse. Soak in solution of ¼ c. (60 ml) ammonia to 1 gal. (3¾ l) water.	Apply enzyme paste. Repeat several times if stain persists. Dry flat in full sun between treatments.	Soak in solution of ¼ c. (60 ml) salt to 2 qts. (2 l) cool water. Rinse. Soak in solution of ¼ c. (60 ml) ammonia to 1 gal. (3¾ l) water. If stain persists, treat with enzyme presoak solution.
Candle-wax:	Remove surface wax with a dull knife.	Place stain between paper towels and press with a warm iron. Replace towels frequently to absorb more wax. Launder with detergent. If traces of color remain, wash again using chlorine bleach.	Same as for bleachables except, to launder replace chlorine bleach with hydrogen peroxide or oxygen bleach after testing fabric.
Catsup, spaghetti or tomato sauce	Scrape off excess. Blot with moist cloth. Repeat until progress stops.	Apply prewash soil & stain remover. Rinse. Repeat. Apply enzyme paste. Rinse; repeat if stain persists. Add vinegar to last rinse.	Blot. Apply absorbent. Repeat. Work in cleaning fluid from underside. Feather edges.
Coffee, tea, chocolate, cocoa	Blot well with damp cloth. Pour cool water through stain if possible.	1) Soak in cool water. Work in detergent. Rinse. If stain remains, apply cleaning fluid. 2) Apply enzyme paste to final traces. Wash in warm water. 3) Force boiling water over stain from arm's length above.	Same as for bleachables.
Cosmetics: makeup, lipstick	Blot well, being careful not to spread stain.	1) Work in cleaning fluid, rubbing toward center. Spot wash with liquid detergent. Rinse. Air dry. 2) Apply prewash soil & stain remover. Blot. Repeat. Rinse with solution of water & a few drops ammonia. Wash in warm water. 3) Soak in enzyme solution for 30 min.	Same as for bleachables.
Crayons: incidental marks	Scrape off excess.	1) Place stain between white tissues or paper towels. Press with warm iron. Pour small amount of cleaning fluid onto absorbent white towel; stroke across stain until stain is gone. 2) Soak in hot enzyme presoak solution for at least 30 min. Rinse.	Same as for bleachables.
Crayons: if washed or dried with clothes	Air dry.	1) Treat at coin-operated drycleaner. 2) Machine-wash with soap (not detergent) & 1 c. (¼ l) baking soda in hottest water safe for fabric. 3) Work in prewash soil & stain remover or soap. Rewash.	Same as for bleachables.
Egg, meat juices & gravy	Moisten with cool water; blot. Repeat.	1) Soak in cool water for 30 min. Work in enzyme paste while wet. Wash in hottest water safe for fabric. 2) Soak in solution of 2 T. (30 ml) enzyme presoak to 1 gal. (3¾ l) water for 30 min.	Same as treatment 1 for bleachables. If stain remains, apply soap (not detergent); wash. Apply prewash soil & stain remover from underside.
Fruit & jelly: fresh	Rinse in cool water; blot. Repeat. Keep moist if possible.	1) Soak in cool water for at least 30 min. or overnight. 2) Work in detergent. Soak in enzyme presoak solution if safe for fabric. Wash in hottest water safe for fabric. 3) Force boiling water through stain from arm's length above. Repeat if stain remains. 4) Work in glycerin. Rinse with prewash soil & stain remover.	Same as treatment 1 for bleachables. If stain remains, work in detergent; wash in warm water. Rinse well.

Spot & Stain Removal

Stain	Pretreatment	Bleachables	Nonbleachables
Fruit & jelly: dried	NOTE: Check citrus stains closely. They may disappear when rinsed & dried. Age & heat bring out yellowing. Once set, they cannot be removed.	1) Apply glycerin to loosen. 2) Apply solution of equal parts alcohol & water. Agitate. Let stand, keeping stain moist. Rinse. Wash, using hottest water safe for fabric.	Same as for bleachables.
Fruit drinks & ices (artificially colored)	Rinse in cool water; blot. Repeat.	Soak in solution of ¼ c. (60 ml) ammonia to 1 qt. (1 l) very warm water for 5 min. Rinse. Repeat until stain is gone. Use solution of ¼ c. (60 ml) vinegar to 2 qts. (2 l) cool water for final rinse.	Same as for bleachables *after testing fabric.*
Grass	None	1) Sponge with rubbing alcohol. (For acetate fabric, dilute alcohol with 2 parts water.) 2) Work in detergent. Rinse twice. 3) Soak in cool enzyme presoak solution for at least 30 min. Rinse. Wash in hottest water safe for fabric.	Same as for bleachables, except soak in enzyme presoak solution for no longer than 30 min. *after testing fabric.* Apply hydrogen peroxide to any remaining stain.
Grease: butter, oils	Scrape off excess. Blot. Apply absorbent. Let stand for several hours.	Apply prewash soil & stain remover; use glycerin or petroleum jelly for stain with dirt. Agitate. Wash in hottest water safe for fabric. If stain remains, use cleaning fluid.	Work in detergent. Wash in warm water. If stain remains, work in cleaning fluid from underside. Apply towel to absorb stain.
Grease: car	Blot. Protect other clothing.	Work in petroleum jelly. Sponge with cleaning fluid. Repeat; rinse well. Wash in hottest water safe for fabric; or use prewash soil & stain remover.	Same as for bleachables.
Gum	Pinch off excess between pieces of fabric or paper towels, being careful not to spread stain.	1) Apply ice to harden stain, or place garment in plastic bag in freezer overnight. Remove loosened part with dull knife. 2) Place stain, face down, on paper towels. Work in cleaning fluid. Pinch off any remaining stain. Sponge with cool water. Wash. Do not machine-dry if *any* stain remains; repeat treatment.	Same as for bleachables.
Ink: ballpoint	Try various solutions because there are different ink formulas. Test solutions on similar fabric. Spray with hairspray. Blot. Rub in detergent. Rinse.	1) Saturate with rubbing alcohol. Agitate; rinse. Air dry. Repeat if progress is made. 2) Treat with permanent press soil & stain remover as directed on package. 3) Apply acetone if safe for fabric. Agitate; rinse.	Same as treatments 1 & 2 for bleachable fabrics.
Ink: felt-tip markers	Do not wash before treating.	Apply acetone, cleaning fluid, alcohol or prewash soil & stain remover until bleeding stops. Air dry. Apply warm glycerin. Agitate. Flush with mild ammonia solution. Wash.	Same as for bleachables.
Mildew	None	Wash in hottest water safe for fabric. If stain remains, soak in solution of ½ c. (120 ml) chlorine bleach to 1 gal. (3¾ l) hot water. Wash; rinse. Dry flat in sun.	NONE
Milk, ice cream, cream, yogurt	Sponge with cool water.	1) Soak in cool water. Apply enzyme paste. Soak in enzyme presoak for at least 30 min. 2) Saturate with prewash soil & stain remover; let stand for 30 min. Wash. 3) Air dry. Apply cleaning fluid to any remaining stain.	Soak in cool water for 30 min. Work in detergent. Air dry. Sponge any remaining stain with cleaning fluid.

Spot & Stain Removal

Stain	Pretreatment	Bleachables	Nonbleachables
Mustard	Scrape off excess.	Apply glycerin. Let stand for 20 to 30 min. Work in liquid soap; let stand for 30 min. Wash in hottest water safe for fabric.	Rinse with solution of equal parts alcohol & water. Apply hydrogen peroxide; rinse.
Nail polish	Lift off excess. Blot well from both sides of fabric.	Work in acetone if safe for fabric, pressing from underside with white cloth or paper towel.	Same as for bleachables if safe for fabric.
Paint: oil-based, fresh	Blot well from both sides of fabric.	Keep from drying by wrapping in plastic. Sponge with cleaning fluid or paint thinner as recommended on paint label. Work in detergent. Rinse. Soak in hot detergent solution overnight. Wash. Air dry.	Same as for bleachables, except soak in warm solution if hot is not safe for fabric. Or apply prewash soil & stain remover.
Paint: oil-based, dried	None	Work in heavy-duty liquid household cleaner. Place in plastic bag; let stand overnight. If paint softens, apply turpentine; blot from both sides of fabric. Remove excess; follow directions for fresh paint, above.	Same as for bleachables.
Paint: water-based	Remove excess. Blot carefully with damp sponge. Rinse sponge; repeat.	1) Spot wash with cool water & detergent. 2) Work in prewash soil & stain remover. Rinse; wash. Air dry. Apply cleaning fluid on any remaining stain.	Same as for bleachables.
Perfume	Sponge with cool water.	Soak in lukewarm water & automatic dishwasher detergent & a few drops white vinegar for 15 min.	Same as for bleachables except use hydrogen peroxide instead of vinegar.
Rust	NOTE: Use rust removers with caution because they contain an acid that can damage the finish on appliances.	1) Apply rust remover as package directs. 2) For large amounts of fabric, use color remover as package directs. 3) For white & light-colored fabrics, apply solution of lemon juice & salt as for set-in stains, below. Lay flat in sun, keep moist.	Use rust remover as directed on package.
Set-in stains (unknown source)	None	For white fabrics, wet stain. Apply lemon juice & salt. Dry flat in sun, adding more solution as fabric dries. Rinse. Wash; repeat treatment if progress is made. Add ½ c. (120 ml) vinegar to rinse.	Soak in solution of 2 T. (30 ml) oxygen bleach to 2 c. (½ l) warm or hot water *after testing fabric.* Cover with damp cloth for several hours. Rinse well.
Tar, asphalt	Scrape off residue with dull knife.	1) Sponge with cleaning fluid, working on underside of stain. Blot, using cloth to absorb as stain releases. Do not wash until stain is completely removed. 2) Apply prewash soil & stain remover as directed on package. Air dry. Repeat until stain is gone. Wash in hot water. Treat any remaining stain with mild chlorine solution.	Same as treatment for bleachable fabrics, except use oxygen bleach instead of chlorine bleach in treatment 2.
Urine	Sponge with cool water.	Soak in cool water. Rinse. Work in detergent. Rinse; air dry. If fabric color has changed, sponge with ammonia. If stain remains, sponge with vinegar.	Same as for bleachables. If ammonia is used on wool, mohair or silk, dilute with equal part water.
Vomit	Sponge with cool water.	Work in liquid detergent; let set for 30 min. Apply a few drops ammonia; flush with tap water. Sponge with solution of ¼ c. (60 ml) salt to 2 qt. (2 l) water, or rinse with water.	Work in enzyme paste. Keep moist. Rinse.

Washing & Drying Clothes

A few minutes of planning before washing and drying saves time in the long run and results in cleaner clothes. Simple preparation can keep you from having to spend time later correcting laundering problems, such as shrinkage, stretching, bleeding, fading, linting, pilling, snags and broken zippers.

Although some garments require hand washing and drip drying, most washable clothing can be machine-laundered. Most washing machines have settings for hot, warm and cold water; permanent press, delicate and normal cycles; and varying water levels for different load sizes. Most home dryers have at least two temperature settings and several cycles that are timed or automatically sensitive to the dryness of the clothes, including an air-dry cycle that tumbles clothes without using heat.

Self-service laundry. Coin-operated washers and dryers are usually large-capacity machines with fewer settings than home machines. However, careful sorting is just as necessary for these large machines as it is at home. Do not combine small loads for washing or drying. Coin-operated dryers often have only a high-temperature setting, so be careful not to overdry garments.

If you regularly use a self-service laundry, set up a basket of supplies to take with you each time. Include detergent, bleaches and other cleaning aids. Also take one or two plastic bags, large enough to hold wet items that cannot be machine-dried.

Home laundry room. A well-stocked laundry room simplifies washing and drying. Basic needs include shelves for supplies, a table for sorting, a clothesline, a wastebasket and plenty of hangers. Have on hand detergents and cleaning agents recommended in the stain removal section. Use a bulletin board to post instructions for garments that need special handling for washing or drying or to alert other family members to special laundry procedures. Also include the following supplies.

- Sewing kit, with several threaded needles, for emergency repairs. Keep one needle threaded with light thread and one with dark.
- Measuring cups and spoons in several sizes for wet and dry ingredients.
- Dishpans or plastic pails in at least two sizes.
- Laundry baskets in various colors or easily identified boxes for each member of the family.

Laundry Tips

Clean the washing machine and remove mineral deposits by filling the washer with warm water and adding ½ gal. (2 l) white vinegar. Then run the wash cycle without any clothing. Pour some of the solution through the fabric softener dispenser.

Keep large quantities of granular detergent in closed plastic containers, such as ice cream buckets. Moisture lessens the cleaning power of detergents. Label the outside of the container with product name.

Save time by adding detergent and filling the machine with water while you are sorting clothes. For best results, add detergent first, then the water. Finally, add the clothes. This spreads the detergent most evenly through the wash water.

Test new garments for colorfastness before washing. Cost is not a guideline to fading because even expensive items may fade. To test, soak garment before washing, or wash it separately.

Test load size in a top-loading washer. Lift the lid and watch the agitation of a small item, such as a blouse. It should surface a minimum of five times in one minute. Otherwise, the load is too large and garments cannot move enough to get clean.

Wash each load for about 8 minutes. Overwashing redeposits soil on clothes. Built-up soil may need up to three washings for complete removal.

Soak heavily soiled items by hand or in the machine.

- To soak by hand, fill a large pail or tub with about 3 qts. (3 l) cool water. Add presoak or 2 T. (30 ml) ammonia (any kind). Add socks, T-shirts and other heavily soiled items or clothes with unpleasant odors. Work them up and down a few times with a plunger or by hand; repeat if necessary. Wring out and wash as usual.

- To soak by machine, fill the washer with cold water to a level that just covers clothes. Add presoak or ¼ c. (60 ml) ammonia and agitate for 5 minutes. Drain water from the machine and wash as usual. Odors and loose soil release better by machine than by hand soaking.

Protect clean light-colored garments with fabric protector such as that used on upholstery. For example, spray a white linen skirt to protect it from stains and soil. This also works well for light-colored canvas shoes.

Machine Washing Procedure

1) Mend any rips, tears, snags or loose buttons before washing clothes to prevent further damage. Empty pockets; close zippers, hooks and buttons to prevent snags. For cleaner collars and cuffs, turn shirts inside out, and button the top button. Loosely tie sashes and drawstrings to prevent tangles.

2) Sort by color. Wash white fabrics separately; they can become dingy when washed with colored items. Separate colorfast items from dark or bright colors that might bleed. Wash similar colors in the same load.

5) Sort by degree of soil. Heavily soiled articles, such as work clothes and children's play clothes, should be washed in a load of similar items. Presoak or pretreat heavily soiled items to keep excess soil out of the wash water.

6) Wash: cold water method. If using granular product, thoroughly dissolve ¼ c. (60 ml) detergent in hot water. Add ¼ c. (60 ml) ammonia; add more ammonia for heavily soiled items. Pour this solution into washer. If using concentrated liquid product, pour 2 T. (3 ml) detergent and ¼ c. (60 ml) ammonia directly into washer. Fill machine with cold water. Add clothes; wash as usual. *Do not use chlorine bleach with ammonia.*

3) Sort by fabric. Separate man-made fibers from natural fibers; man-made fibers attract oils released from natural fibers. These oils build up, especially on set-in stains, making spots more noticeable after several washings. Separate fabrics that require a delicate cycle such as knits, laces and sheers. Also, separate heavy lint-shedders, such as fleece and terrycloth, from smooth-surfaced fabrics.

4) Sort by bulk. Items need enough space in the washer to move freely. One king or queen-size sheet, a single sheet and a few small items make up a load for an average-size washer.

7) Wash: warm or hot water method. Heavily soiled or greasy clothes are most effectively cleaned in warm or hot water. Treat greasy areas of fabric with a heavy-duty liquid household cleaner or ammonia before laundering. Measure detergent and ammonia as for cold water method; put each directly into tub of machine. Fill washer with warm or hot water, then add clothes, and wash as usual.

8) Rinse. Film left on clothing fibers after washing dulls colors and turns whites dingy or yellow. To cut soapy residue, add ¼ c. (60 ml) white vinegar to rinse cycle. Add vinegar through fabric softener dispenser. If you have used too much detergent, causing too many suds in the washer, add up to 1 c. (¼ l) vinegar to each load. Vinegar will not leave an odor in clothes.

Machine Drying

For best drying results, leave room in the dryer for clothes to tumble loosely. Crowding clothes slows down the drying process, uses more fuel or energy, and causes wrinkles.

Leave clothes in the dryer only long enough to remove moisture and wrinkles. Overdrying causes shrinkage, heat-set wrinkles and static cling. If possible, remove clothes from dryer while they are still slightly damp. Have a supply of hangers handy to hang clothes as they come out of the dryer.

Shake each item after removing it from the washer, whether it is to be dried in the machine or on a clothesline. The dryer can more efficiently dry clothes with loose wrinkles than clothes tightly twisted from the spin cycle of the washing process.

Sort items into small loads, according to weight. Sorting saves time in the long run because it prevents further wrinkling, gives better results and reduces the amount of ironing necessary. For example, do not put heavy towels and lightweight lingerie in the same load for the dryer, even though they may have been washed in one load.

Sort permanent press and wash-and-wear items into small loads separate from other clothes. To eliminate ironing, dry three to five shirts and/or blouses at a time for 3 to 5 minutes. Remove two and keep the rest tumbling while you hang the first two. Remove the others, toss in five more, and repeat.

Use short cycle and low heat for lingerie and knits. Remove lingerie while it's still damp. Let it finish drying on hangers or a clothesline. Knits should be dried carefully to prevent shrinkage, or dried flat on an absorbent towel.

Use short cycle and no heat for vinyl, rubber and rubber-backed items. Plastic items, such as tablecloths and baby pants, should be left in the dryer no more than 5 minutes. Remove immediately, shake, and hang or fold. When left in the dryer, they may stiffen or become wrinkled.

Do not machine-dry silk, fiberglass or wool. As a safety precaution, wash clothes that have been treated with drycleaning solvent before machine drying them. Use low heat to machine-dry bras or similar items with large areas of elastic.

Remove lint from the dryer frequently, twice during the cycle for heavy loads. A clean lint filter increases the efficiency of the dryer, uses less energy and shortens the automatic cycles. A clogged filter is not only inefficient, but a fire hazard. Also check the outside dryer vent to be sure it is not clogged by lint or an animal's nest.

Laundry Mishaps

Prevent laundry mishaps by paying special attention to care labels, using the washer and dryer properly, and taking time to remedy common problems. Even with the most careful procedures, however, some laundry problems may occur.

Shrinkage. To avoid, follow care labels closely. Be especially careful to avoid high temperatures for washing and drying. Also use slow agitation for machine washing. Once a garment has shrunk, restretching it to its original size may be impossible.

Stretching. Some acrylic knits stretch easily out of shape because of the process used to dye them. For acrylic knits that are stretched out of shape, reshape by moistening with a steam iron; then block and pin to ironing board or a towel until dry.

Color problems. Graying and yellowing of fabrics can mean that you need to change washing procedures. Graying can be caused by improper sorting, too little detergent, lack of hot water, hard water, oversized wash load or insufficient soaking. During the washing process, clothing can also become dingy if rinsing does not immediately follow washing; dirt can resettle onto the fabric. Yellowing can be caused by body oils in fabric, minerals in water, too much fabric softener and natural aging.

Restore whiteness to fabric yellowed from body oils by washing with hottest water safe for fabric. Add 1 cup (¼ l) chlorine bleach after agitating clothes for 4 minutes. Agitate for 4 more minutes, then soak for 15 minutes. Restart washer for regular cycle; repeat entire process until yellowing disappears.

If a fabric is yellowed from minerals in the water, you may need to filter or treat the water supply to prevent further staining. To remove mineral spots, hold stained area over a pan of boiling water and

squeeze lemon juice on spots. To treat overall yellowing from minerals, launder with fabric rust remover if safe for fabric. Do not use chlorine bleach because it will only worsen the stain.

Soaking fabrics for several hours or overnight also whitens them. Add ½ c. (120 ml) chlorine bleach and ½ c. (120 ml) automatic dishwasher detergent to a large bucket of hot water. After solution has cooled, soak white clothes for 3 to 4 hours. For nonbleachable fabrics, soak overnight in a solution of 1 gal. (3¾ l) hot water and 1 to 2 t. (5 to 10 ml) cream of tartar. After soaking, wash clothes as usual.

Linting. Some fabrics naturally produce lint during washing and drying; however, you may be able to control the amount of lint produced. Excessive linting may be caused by improper sorting, overloading the washer or too little detergent. To remove lint from clothing, put the garment through the wash cycle again, using fabric softener in the rinse. Residue that looks like lint may be caused by undissolved fabric softener or detergent, or nonphosphate granular detergent.

Pilling. Little balls of fabric may appear on the surface of acrylic and polyester garments. To prevent pilling, turn garment inside out before machine-laundering, and use slower agitation and short cycles for washing and drying. Use a disposable razor to remove pills from smooth-textured knits. Or, pull fabric taut over a curved surface and carefully cut off pills with sharp trimmers or embroidery scissors.

Snags, pulled buttons and broken zippers. To prevent these problems, mend clothing and fasten all closures before washing. Turn knits and items with intricate trim inside out to prevent snagging.

Hand Washing & Drip Drying

Care labels may specify hand washing for delicate items or garments that might shrink or stretch out of shape, such as sweaters, knits, silks and wools. Fabric, garment construction and trimmings can affect whether an item should be hand washed.

Pretreat all spots and stains. Then, fill a dishpan or sink with coolest water that will remove soil. Add mild soap or detergent. Thoroughly mix detergent in water before adding clothes.

Add clothes and allow them to soak if heavily soiled. Squeeze suds gently through garment without rubbing fabric layers against each other. Rubbing can transfer stains. Rely on detergent and water to clean garment, rather than vigorous scrubbing.

Rinse several times without wringing or twisting. Use cool water to reduce wrinkles. To dry knits, roll in a towel to blot; then lay flat, blocking to original shape.

Drip drying reduces wrinkling without the risk of shrinkage from heat. Care labels may recommend drip drying for fabrics such as acetate, cotton, rayon, and permanent press blends or finishes.

How to Drip Dry Garments

1) Hang garment on rust-proof hanger without removing excess water. To speed drying, blot with a towel, but do not squeeze, wring or crease the garment. Fasten zippers and other closures, especially the top button on a dress, shirt or blouse.

2) Straighten lines of garment and grainlines of fabric to hang evenly. Side seams should be vertical, and waistline or hemline should be horizontal. Smooth stitching with fingers to eliminate puckering, especially on collar, seams and plackets.

Ironing & Pressing

Ironing and pressing not only reduce wrinkles in clothing, but also help to retain details of tailoring, such as creased pants legs, smooth plackets and crisp pleats. With modern synthetic fibers and blends, ironing is not the chore it used to be; however, pressing and ironing are still a routine part of clothing care.

Care labels can help you determine the amount of ironing needed. For minimum ironing, choose synthetic fabrics and soft styles.

Use laundering techniques to reduce wrinkling. Do not wring or twist garments before drip drying. Remove clothes from an automatic dryer before they are completely dry; hang them immediately.

Ironing is gliding the iron across the fabric; pressing is raising and lowering the iron onto the fabric without any gliding motion. Iron with straight strokes, lengthwise or crosswise to the grain of the fabric. Diagonal or circular strokes can stretch the fabric. Use a pressing technique for details.

Organize routine ironing by beginning with garments requiring the lowest steam setting. Then empty the iron for garments that need to be ironed with dry heat.

When ironing or pressing garments avoid wrinkling parts that have already been ironed. After ironing the garment, touch up important parts, such as the collar and cuffs. Be sure ironed clothing is dry and cool before storing.

Ironing & Pressing Tips

Prevent ironshine by using a press cloth or soleplate cover. Or use light pressure on the wrong side of the fabric. Ironshine occurs most often on dark colors and thickly layered areas.

Do not press or iron clothes that are dirty or stained. Heat will set the stains.

Press napped fabrics carefully to avoid crushing the nap. Place the garment, wrong side up, over a thick towel. Use steam and apply little pressure.

Keep a pump-spray bottle of water handy for misting stubborn wrinkles or creases.

Clean the iron and wash the ironing board cover often to avoid transferring soil to clothes. Put the cover on the ironing board while still damp from the washer; allow to dry in place to shrink-fit.

Use a hand-held steamer for quick touch-ups.

Smooth the surface of your iron by placing a brown paper bag on the ironing board with a piece of waxed paper on top. Pass the medium-warm iron quickly across the waxed paper.

Scorch can sometimes be removed, but it is best to prevent it in the first place. Do not use an iron that is too hot and never allow the iron to rest in one place on the fabric. To remove light scorch, sponge with a solution of one part hydrogen peroxide to 20 parts water. For wool, add a few drops of ammonia. Place a white towel under scorched area. Allow solution to soak in for a few minutes, then move treated area to a dry section of the towel and rinse with clear water.

How to Clean an Iron

Remove starch or sizing buildup. Pour a capful of ammonia on a damp washcloth; fold cloth twice to provide eight fresh sides. Stroke medium-hot iron across cloth, rotating iron slowly to release residue from the bottom. Turn soiled corner back and repeat. To keep from breathing the strong ammonia fumes, do not stand directly over the iron.

Remove melted plastic. Set iron at low temperature and rub with a soft cloth. For tougher buildup, rub with fine steel wool. Do not allow the iron to become hot. To remove tough, gummy buildup, use oven cleaner. Let oven cleaner set for up to 5 minutes; then wipe with a paper towel. Repeat if necessary.

Drycleaning

Drycleaning uses solvents containing little or no water. These solvents dissolve grease and oil without penetrating the fibers as washing does. Charcoal derivatives and sizing added to the solvent remove odor, reduce discoloration, and restore body and crispness to fabrics.

Clean garments regularly because stains and soil left too long may be impossible to remove. Tell the drycleaner the source of any stains, especially sugar-based stains like white wine and ginger ale, so they can be pretreated. If not treated before the drycleaning process, heat from drying and pressing may set the stain.

Unless a label specifies DO NOT DRYCLEAN, most garments can be safely drycleaned. Clothing should always be taken to a full-service drycleaner when DRYCLEAN PROFESSIONALLY is stated on the care label. Also consider drycleaning for

- delicate fabrics such as silk and chiffon.
- large, greasy stains that would require large amounts of drycleaning fluid if treated at home.
- tailored items that require professional pressing and steaming after cleaning.
- garments that are going into long-term storage.
- clothing that needs a finish restored.
- stains that have not been removed after several attempts, or if a test of the stain-removal fluid on a hidden seam shows that the home remedy destroys the fabric dye or finish.
- garments without care labels when you are not sure of the fiber content and you do not want to risk washing.

Clean all parts and accessories of a matching suit or outfit at once, even if only one piece needs cleaning. This ensures that any color change will be uniform.

Even with the most careful drycleaning procedures, some stains are impossible to remove, dyes may run or fade, or fabrics may shrink. Drycleaning reduces the risk of these hazards, but the cleaner is not responsible for a manufacturer's poor workmanship or owner's neglect. Worn areas or small holes that were not obvious in the garment before cleaning may become apparent after cleaning.

When choosing a drycleaner, select one who is a member of a professional cleaners' organization. Use a telephone directory which lists the cleaners' services, or ask for recommendations from friends. Before taking clothing to a drycleaner the first time, ask the cleaner about available services, stain treatment and complaint procedures.

Three Types of Drycleaning

Full service provides professional expertise and pretreatment of soiled areas, spot and stain removal, solvent cleaning, lint removal and complete pressing. Sometimes it also includes minor repairs. Garments are returned in plastic bags and on hangers. Pricing is by the piece.

Bulk-cleaned garments are priced by weight, with several garments weighed together. Soiled areas are pretreated before solvent cleaning. This method does not include pressing or spot removal. Garments are returned covered with plastic and on hangers.

Coin-operated drycleaning machines provide a do-it-yourself method, priced by the load. Sort garments by light and dark colors before cleaning; process each group separately. This method does not include pressing, stain removal or hangers.

How to Prepare Garments for Drycleaning

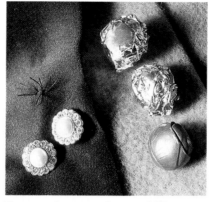

Empty pockets of money, keys, candy and gum, facial tissues, handkerchiefs, ink and marking pens, and paper items. These articles can cause lint, color blotches, sticky masses and fabric damage. Check hems and cuffs for stray items.

Remove buttons that could be damaged, or cover them with foil. Solvent can weaken glue holding stones in buttons and can melt or break some plastic buttons. Remove leather buttons from non-leather garments to keep them from getting scratched or discolored.

Examine seams and make needed repairs. Secure loose belt carriers and shoulder pads. Repair broken zippers and worn or split seams. Reattach loose buttons that could fall off. Identify unrepaired areas to drycleaner before cleaning.

Special Drycleaner Services

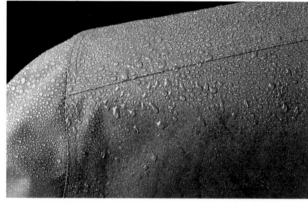

Water-repellent finish on raincoats and outerwear causes water to bead and roll off fabric surface, but it does not totally prevent saturation. It also provides some soil-resistance to retard soiling and reduce frequency of cleanings.

Storage containers are provided for bridal gowns and formal wear, which are packed in acid-free tissue that prevents discoloration and deterioration.

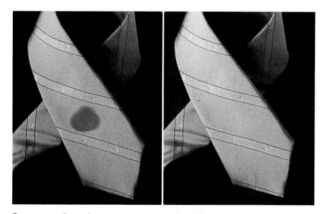

Spots and stains are removed with steam-activated chemical compounds and methods to minimize fabric damage.

Blocking of knit and crocheted garments to size or specified measurements gives a finished look to hand-made garments.

Fabrics that Need Special Handling

Some fabrics require special care for cleaning. For these, the usual process of washing or drycleaning may have to be altered, or a special cleaning process may be necessary.

Follow care label instructions closely. You may be able to clean or launder the garment yourself, or it may require professional care. Some garments and fabrics are so sensitive to available cleaning methods that a signed waiver will be requested, relieving the professional drycleaner from the responsibility of any resulting damage.

Dryclean deep-colored garments, dark prints, loosely woven fabrics, brocade, chiffon, metallics, taffeta, satin and charmeuse. Dryclean suits because of inner construction. Blot liquid spills, then take the garment to the drycleaner for spot removal, identifying the stain to the drycleaner. You may damage the fabric surface if you try to remove the stain.

Leather must be cleaned by a special leather process to keep the hide from shrinking, and to protect its softness and color. Garments with dark leather trimming require the leather cleaning process to keep trims from bleeding. Avoid storing leather in plastic covers to allow the leather to breathe.

Suede, which is leather that has been split and brushed, can be cleaned and cared for in the same way as leather. To remove surface soil and renew texture, brush with a wire suede brush or dry sponge.

Synthetic suedes can be machine washed and dried unless the lining material or garment construction requires drycleaning. If the garment is washable, use warm water and avoid overdrying. Spot-clean with warm water and a sponge, then brush lightly with a soft-bristled brush. Press on the wrong side, using a cool iron and the right side of a napped press cloth.

Synthetic leather and vinyls become stiff from drycleaning. To clean, sponge the surface with warm soapy water, rinse with clear water and pat dry. Some synthetic leather labels recommend drycleaning; however, the drycleaner may request a signed waiver.

Bonded fabrics have a lining or foam layer, or both, laminated to the back for stability or warmth. Bonding may separate in the drycleaning process, and foam backings may crumble after repeated cleanings. Identify bonded fabrics to the drycleaner so lower heat settings will be used.

Down garments remain attractive and hold their warmth longer when drycleaned instead of washed. They may not be able to withstand the agitation in home washers; channel or quilting threads may break, down may shift or work through the garment, oil from the down may stain the garment shell, and detergent may streak the fabric because adequate rinsing is difficult. Drycleaners can restore a water repellent finish. Clean garments at least once during the season and before storage.

Silk may usually be hand washed in lukewarm water with a mild detergent. Rinse in cool water, roll in a towel to remove excess moisture and press immediately with a cool iron. However, shrinkage can occur with washing unless the fabric was preshrunk by the same method. When sewing with silk, always preshrink the fabric.

Watermarks and color loss are caused by water, perspiration, alcohol, light and abrasion. To keep silk looking its best, wear dress shields, store away from direct sunlight and clean frequently. Drycleaning can sometimes restore slight loss of luster or color.

Sequins can melt, discolor, curl or become brittle and break when drycleaned. Remove sequin trimmings from the garment before cleaning; reattach after cleaning. Some sequins can withstand drycleaning; however, the cleaner may request a signed waiver.

Fur is cleaned only with fur method by a professional drycleaner. The garments are tumbled in a dry compound saturated with solvents to remove grease and oil. Avoid cleaning too frequently; once every one or two years is adequate, depending on the fur and usage. To keep the hide from drying out during warm weather, store fur in a vault with controlled humidity and temperature of about 50° to 55°F (10° to 13°C). Fur storage is available from a bonded furrier.

Synthetic fur has the appearance of fur but is produced from man-made fibers. Fur method is the preferred cleaning method because normal drycleaning solvents and high heat may cause loss of luster and softness. To store, cover with paper or fabric bag and hang. Avoid plastic bags unless the garment is first covered with cotton sheeting.

Closets

The long life and fresh appearance of clothing depends on proper storage as well as proper cleaning. How you handle your clothes from day to day, how you store out-of-season clothing and how you pack for travel affect the life and look of your wardrobe.

Organization is the key to keeping clothes neat and in good condition. Clothing in a properly organized closet maintains its shape, stays clean and unwrinkled, and saves you time and energy. Use your existing closet space to its fullest potential with closet accessories and hardware to expand the available space.

Out-of-season clothes have their own special storage needs. Prepare these garments properly to protect them from moths, mildew and staining.

Packing for wrinkle-free travel requires special techniques. When you arrive at your destination, clothing should be easily accessible and ready to wear.

Daily Care

Proper day-to-day handling of clothing extends the life of the garment by prolonging the time between each washing or drycleaning.

- Handle garments gently. Remove from hangers with care to avoid broken zippers and rips.

- Rotate clothing use over a few days, allowing moisture to evaporate and wrinkles to hang out before wearing again.

- Air and brush clothing, especially wool garments, after wearing. Remove spots immediately to postpone drycleaning.

- Use tubular plastic, padded or wood hangers to help clothes maintain their shape. Wire hangers can bend and sag, rust, cause snags, and leave dents in shoulders.

- To keep the shape of special blouses, dresses and jackets, stuff the arms with used drycleaning bags.

- Do not hang or store clothing near a heat source.

- Before hanging garments, remove items from pockets and close fasteners (buttons, snaps, zippers and hooks) to avoid wrinkling and help garment maintain shape.

- Be sure that everything in your closet fits, needs no repair, and receives regular wear.

Organizing a Closet

Install a system that accommodates your wardrobe without being too elaborate for your needs. For example, a woman's wardrobe of dresses requires a different set-up from a man's closet of suits, yet a shared closet will need to be adapted to both needs.

People who are naturally organized will want a compartment for each clothing category, such as dresses, pants and blouses, with a place for every accessory or article of clothing. For others, an easier way of storage is to divide the closet into only three or four major clothing and accessory categories.

Whatever your goal for a well-organized closet, there are four main principles of closet organization you can put to use in any storage area of your home.

Four Principles of Closet Organization

Keep items within easy reach. Avoid high shelves or low drawers for frequently used clothing. Keep a low, sturdy stool nearby for reaching high shelves.

Keep items clearly visible. Use clear plastic storage containers, wire mesh baskets and open shelves so that garments are easy to see.

Store similar items together. Hang and store similar items in the same area. To make accessorizing easier, keep jewelry, scarves and belts near clothing.

Divide and compartmentalize space. Divide space in the closet into smaller categories, designating a place for each type of item, such as skirts, dresses, jackets and accessories.

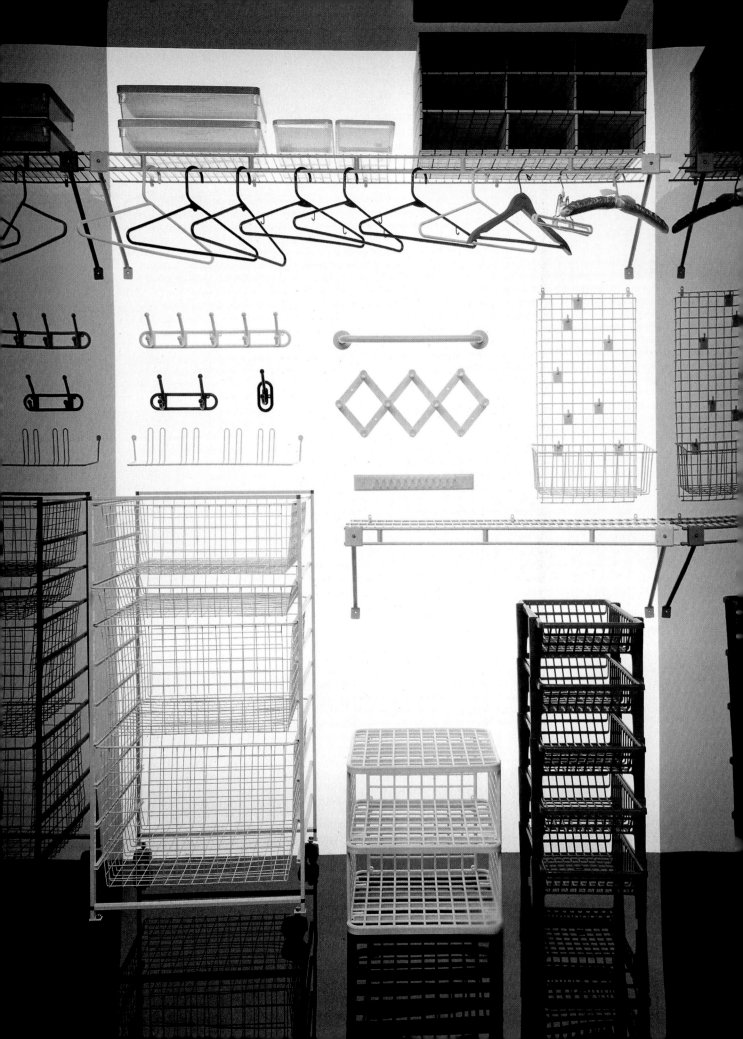

Closet Hardware

Items that aid closet organization are available in notions departments, hardware stores, variety stores and specialty shops at a price to suit any budget. They are usable in any combination to meet your individual needs without the expense of custom built-ins. Many closet hardware items are portable, so they can be used in any type of closet and altered to meet a changing lifestyle.

Double rods expand the available space for hanging clothes in a closet. Most closets are equipped with only one rod at a height of 60" (150 cm). Raise one pole to 80" (200 cm) and install a second pole 40" (100 cm) from the floor. For longer garments, such as coats and dresses, extend the lower rod across only part of the closet width to leave hanging room from the upper rod. You can also buy poles that attach to and hang from the upper rod.

Shelves are used to store clothes such as sweaters, shorts, T-shirts and accessories. Store hats on upper shelves and shoes on lower shelves.

Tubular plastic hangers hold clothes in shape better than wire hangers. Use sturdy wooden hangers for coats and heavy suit jackets. Padded hangers hold the shape of lightweight silky blouses and other fine-fabric clothing. Use single skirt and pants hangers to keep garments easily accessible and wrinkle-free.

Plastic hooks can be placed anywhere in your closet to be used for hats, belts, jewelry, bags, robes and pajamas.

Kitchen towel racks can be hung on the wall or back of a closet door for accessories such as scarves and ties.

Mugracks hang vertically or horizontally for an easy-to-install method of organizing jewelry, scarves, ties, belts and small purses.

Man's tie and belt rack can also be used in a woman's closet for ties, lingerie, leotards and belts.

Grids help organize accessories on the wall or back of the closet door. Attach hooks and baskets to hold jewelry, scarves, stockings.

Clear plastic boxes keep items such as emergency mending supplies, jewelry, belts, shoes, and sweaters organized and dust-free.

Shoe racks create storage for several pairs of shoes and can be used on the wall or back of a door. Overhead shoe chests are used to store occasionally used shoes and hangbags.

Wire basket drawers in a closet eliminate cramped bureau drawers. You can see underwear, stockings, handbags and sweaters at a glance. Air circulation keeps clothes fresh, preventing odors and mildew.

Open plastic bins stack to hold shoes, accessories and underwear. Anything stored in bins is easily accessible and visible.

Closet Design

Man's closet. Two-pole design doubles space. Use wire mesh basket drawers for underwear, socks and foldable clothing. Shelf holds sweaters and hats. Rack on door organizes shoes. Tie rack and mirror are handy on closet door. Use wood hangers for jackets and suits; use pants hangers for trousers.

To be convenient for each family member, closets for men, women and children may differ in design and organization. Once you have designed closets to suit the needs of each family member, keeping clothes organized becomes easier.

Before you begin organizing a closet, take an inventory of what is now in it. This inventory will guide your selection of hardware and help you evaluate the clothing items that belong in your wardrobe, or the wardrobe of other family members. Reevaluate the closet every six months or seasonally.

Start with a sketch of the closet, and draw the design that best suits your needs. With a little planning and a few household tools you can easily transform a closet.

- Use two rods if your wardrode consists mostly of separates.

- Allow space for dresses, robes and gowns.

- Provide open space for shoes and accessories.

- Duplicate storage areas if closet is shared.

- Bifold doors make it easier to see everything in the closet at one time. If you have sliding doors, group similar items behind one door so you can get an entire outfit together at one end of the closet. Use the back of a standard door for added storage.

- Keep a separate laundry bag for clothes that will need special laundry attention, such as hand washables or items that are washed separately.

Woman's walk-in closet. Three-pole design expands space and keeps clothes from being crushed. Use drawer unit for foldable clothes and stackables, such as flat purses. Lower deep drawer is a laundry basket. Shelving holds sweaters, hats, and purses. Baskets and hooks organize accessories.

Children's shared closet. Teach children to care for their own clothing, by designating space for each item in their closets. Two-pole design doubles space and separates dress clothes from play clothes. Inexpensive plastic bins and easy-to-handle tubular hangers are a different color for each child. Open design of bins makes it easy to see and reach shoes, underwear and foldable clothing. Use top shelf for storing out-of-season clothing.

Storing Seasonal Clothing

Clothing that is seasonal or worn only occasionally requires special care to prevent damage from moths, mildew and discoloration. After properly cleaning garments to prepare them for storage, choose storage areas, containers and packing materials that offer the best protection. When the seasons change, you can unpack your favorite winter sweaters or summer shorts from storage and find them clean and ready to wear.

Moths. Detecting moths before damage occurs is difficult. The best way to ensure against moths is to clean the clothing before storage and then put it in a sealed trunk, box or closet with moth balls or crystals. Use 1 pound (450 g) of moth balls for every 100 cubic feet (3 cu m) of space. Vapors release downward, so hang cloth bags of the product from the top of the storage enclosure. Seal space with tape, including the cracks around closets, for one or two days while extermination takes place.

Place herbal sachets with the mothballs. They cover the mothball odor with a pleasant fragrance and help to repel moths. To make an herbal sachet, use 1 ounce (30 g) each of cedar chips, bay leaf, lavender, patchouli and rosemary. Add a pinch of whole cloves. Mix ingredients together and divide into five or six sachet bags. Use one bag in a drawer, two bags in a small closet, or four bags in a walk-in closet.

Mildew. Mildew is a mold that weakens and destroys natural fibers and discolors synthetics. In a humid climate, mildew can form in just one day.

To prevent mildew, make sure all clothing is completely dry before storing. Press garments with a hot iron to remove all dampness. Do not use starch or sizing on clothing to be stored because mildew is especially attracted to the protein in these products. Avoid using plastic bags that trap moisture. Hang cloth bags of chemical desiccants (moisture absorbers such as silica gel and calcium chloride) in storage areas. Or place containers of desiccants on shelves, but avoid direct contact with clothing. When the weather is dry, air out storage spaces.

Discoloration. Stains can seem to mysteriously appear after long-term storage. Before clothing is packed away, it must be completely free from dirt, body oils, perfume, starch, sizing, fabric softeners, soap and hard water deposits. These can cause discoloration and stains. Use a mild dishwashing detergent and soft water to clean washables for storage. If necessary, add a water softener to your wash. Dryclean all other garments.

Storage Areas

Clothing storage can vary in time from a few months to many years. Seasonal clothing is often stored for up to six months at a time. Holiday or theatrical costumes may be packed away for a year. Maternity and baby clothes may be stored for several years. Special consideration must be given to the storage of heirloom and sentimental favorites, such as wedding dresses and gowns, which may be stored for many years.

Store clothing in an area where the temperature and humidity do not reach extremes. Basements, attics and garages expose clothing to dampness, extreme temperatures, dust, grease or fumes, which can damage fibers. Rely instead on out-of-the-way areas such as back shelves of a closet or under the bed.

Trunks or suitcases. When trunks or suitcases are not in use for traveling, they can serve as storage containers. Before storing items in a suitcase, fold them and slip them into a pillowcase. Then you can easily remove them without disturbing their arrangement when the suitcase is needed for a trip.

Garment bags. If seasonal garments are stored in a closet, cover them with cloth garment bags. Most full-service drycleaners also offer storage of seasonal garments as one of their services.

Boxes. To save space, use boxes that are the same size so they will stack evenly on top of one another. Corrugated plastic boxes are lightweight, but sturdier than cardboard and will last for years. Available in assorted sizes and colors, they are waterproof and vented for long-term storage. Label boxes with detachable cards.

Cedar chests and closets. Cedar enclosures are effective against moths and insects if they are tightly constructed of cedar heartwood at least ¾" (2 cm) thick. The oil from the heartwood kills moth larvae; odor alone does not repel moths. Line cedar chests with acid-free paper or muslin sheeting to protect clothing from resin and wood acid.

Besides traditional cedar closets and chests, portable cedar containers are available. Canvas garment bags with a cedar top and bottom are for closet storage; canvas sweater and blanket bags with a cedar bottom are for shelf or under-the-bed storage.

Packing materials. Because natural fibers need to breathe, clothing should not be stored in air-tight plastic for an extended period. Instead, wrap garments in muslin sheeting or acid-free paper, which can be purchased in art supply and framing stores. Also use paper or muslin to line chests, drawers and shelves because wood and metal surfaces may stain clothing.

Packing for Travel

On-the-road clothing care starts with careful packing to protect clothes, make them easily accessible and keep them wrinkle-free. A suitcase is really a traveling closet, so the principles of closet organization apply when planning your packing. Put items you will need first in a small tote or near the top of your suitcase.

Pack clothing in layers, interlocking the items to prevent wrinkles and sliding, as shown on page 46. When packing a suitcase, place each garment in the case with the end extending outside the case. Layer garments with the ends extending in alternating directions. Interlock clothing by folding the ends of the garments over each other. To prevent crushed clothing, place heavy items, such as hair dryers, cosmetics cases and shoes, along the hinged side of the case. When the suitcase is upright, the bulky items will be on the bottom.

Use the interlocking method to pack soft-sided totes, but fold and interlock clothes *before* placing them in the tote. Roll knits and other casual items, and pack them into corners of the tote. Pack tightly to avoid wrinkling; when every corner of space is used, clothing cannot slide and get unwanted creases.

Packing Tips

Small items. Place socks, hose and other small items in the toes of shoes to save space and help retain the shape of the shoe.

Shoes. Cover shoes with fabric shoe mittens to protect them from marks and scratches and to keep them from soiling other items.

Lingerie. Fold slips, panties, bras and other undergarments in thirds and roll together in sets. Pack in a plastic bag, which can serve as a laundry bag on the return trip.

Men's underwear and socks. Pack as a set. Fold undershorts and shirts together, lengthwise in thirds. Roll up with socks on outside so they can later be matched with outfits.

Nightgowns, pajamas and robes. Fold garments lengthwise in thirds and roll up. Tuck rolled sets in corners of suitcase.

Belts. Place along sides of the suitcase. To prevent cracking, do not roll.

Cosmetics and toiletries. Pack in a plastic bag with a tight seal to protect clothes from accidental leakage. Buy products in the travel size or transfer to small plastic bottles to save space.

Gowns and evening wear. Before folding, lay tissue paper or plastic drycleaner bags on garments to provide padding and prevent sharp creases. Cover folded garments with paper or drycleaner bags to protect against soiling.

Tissue paper. Stuff into jacket sleeves to keep them from wrinkling. Tissue paper, a plastic drycleaning bag, or a small folded item such as a T-shirt can be placed between folds of garments to prevent creases.

Clothing Care Supplies for Travelers

Do not wait to get home to treat stains or spots on clothing. The longer a spot goes without treatment, the less chance there is of completely removing it. Pack a bottle of stain remover for permanent press fabrics to take oil spots out of polyester and synthetics. For stains on clothes that need drycleaning, bring a bottle of cleaning fluid spot remover. A readily available first aid for many spots is club soda. Include a small bottle of mild detergent for hand washables. To freshen clothing and remove wrinkles, hang garments in the bathroom when bathing or taking a shower.

Pack a small travel sewing kit for emergency repairs. A variety of sewing kits for traveling are available in department, drug and fabric stores. Or make your own to include

- one or two hand sewing needles,
- several basic colors of thread wrapped around a piece of cardboard,
- needle threader for repairing knit snags,
- glue stick for emergency tacking,
- safety pins,
- folding scissors, and
- buttons.

Folding Clothes for Packing

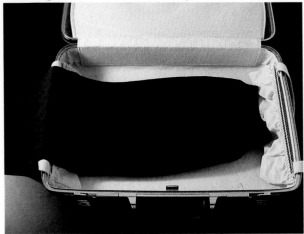

Pants. Fold lengthwise along creases, with fly unzipped. Place waistband against side of suitcase and seat of pants toward hinges.

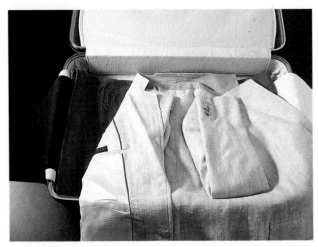

Jackets and coats. Lay jacket, lining side down, with lapels and collar spread flat. Fold shoulders to meet at center back seam, then fold sleeves up at elbows. Fold sides of jacket back so lapels almost meet.

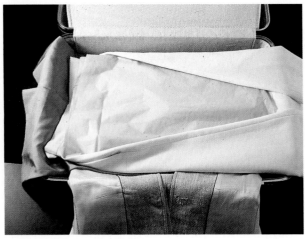

Skirts. Lay skirt face down and cover with tissue paper. Fold sides to center, if necessary, to make a long straight rectangle.

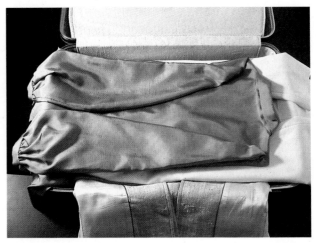

Shirts and blouses. Fasten every other button; fold shirt back at shoulders. Fold sleeves back with cuffs pointing to shirttail.

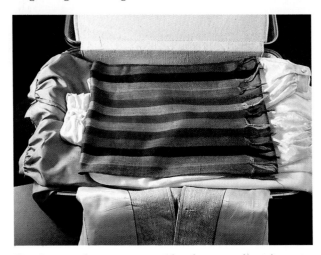

Continue to layer garments in alternate directions before folding them across the middle. Place the more delicate garments on top.

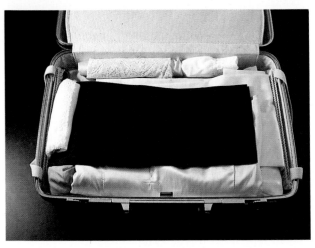

Interlock garments by folding ends into suitcase one by one; smooth out wrinkles as you fold. Place small items in corners to prevent garments from sliding.

Packing a Soft-sided Tote

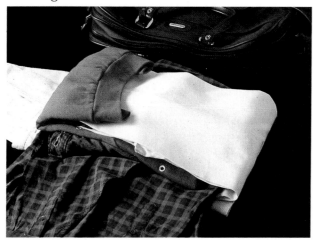

Fold and interlock clothing on a flat surface using the interlocking method described on opposite page. Fold clothing to fit the width of tote. Place this bundle in tote.

Roll knit garments, including sweaters, underwear, socks, knit pants and skirts. To roll, lay garment flat, line with tissue paper and fold lengthwise into thirds. Roll up, smoothing creases as you go. Pack tightly into corners of tote.

Packing a Garment Bag

Lay garment bag flat. Hang jackets, shirts, dresses and pants on hangers. Fold sleeves in as necessary.

Fold up long garments at bottom to prevent wrinkling. Smooth clothes carefully.

Repair

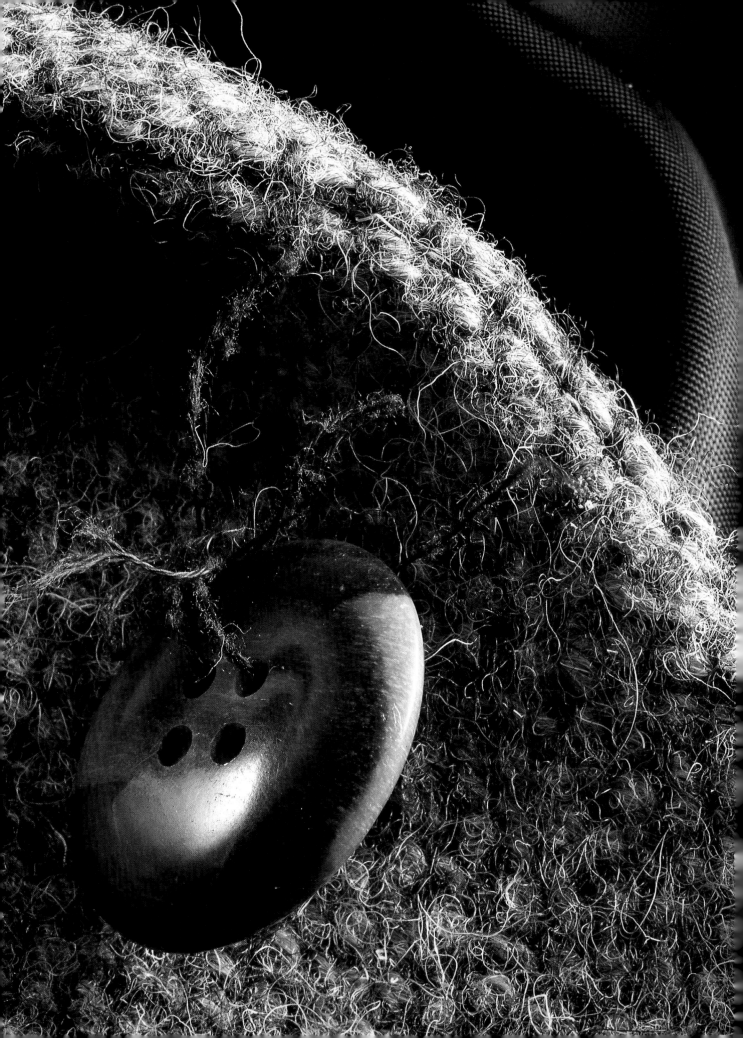

Clothing Repairs

The reward of mending a favorite skirt or repairing a child's outfit for another season of wear is more than a financial savings. You will feel a great deal of personal satisfaction from making a repair that is so inconspicuous no one will notice it, or from making a patch that is so creative it enhances the look of the original garment.

Mending includes all types of repairs to damaged garments. Threads weaken, seams split and elastic stretches to its limit in well-worn garments that may still have years of use except for these minor signs of wear. Elbows and knees of shirts and pants may wear thin from normal use. Poor fit may cause a seam to split or a zipper to break. Faulty manufacturing may result in a raveled hem, lost button or broken topstitching. An accidental fall or a snag on a sharp point can turn a brand new garment into an item that needs repair before it can be worn again.

Some repairs can be avoided with preventive mending. Reinforce or strengthen areas that receive stress and hard wear before the damage occurs, or before the weak areas wear through completely. The smaller the repair, the less time it will take to mend. It's easier to iron a patch on the back of thinly worn pants knees than to wait until the threads tear and the fabric has to be repaired.

New sewing notions make mending and preventive mending simpler and less time-consuming than ever before. Many of these items are iron-on or fusible, or require only basic sewing skills. In addition, hand-held mending appliances and portable mending machines make it possible for anyone to quickly make sturdy basic repairs, even without a sewing machine.

Make mending fun by using a little imagination. For example, patches are not the only way to repair a tear or hole. A strategically placed pocket, row of trim, applique (purchased or designed yourself), decorative button or non-functional zipper may be just the thing to creatively conceal a torn area or reinforce a worn spot.

Before beginning a project, take into account costs in time and money for repairing a garment versus buying a replacement. Once you decide to do the repair, consider the repair alternatives and the time and skills required for each.

As in any craft, there are special tools and equipment that are essential to professional results. Finally, remember that besides the right tools, a positive attitude and comfortable work area with good lighting contribute as much as sewing ability to the success of a repair.

Mending Tools

Keep sewing equipment together so mending and repair work can be done efficiently. Organize equipment in a portable box or basket which can be carried to a comfortable chair in a well-lit area. Also, for preventive mending, keep a basic repair kit handy in the laundry area.

Common mending equipment and notions have been divided into three types of kits: the basic kit and family kit for hand mending, and the sewing-machine-plus kit. To assemble your mending

kit, choose the items that are appropriate for the mending tasks you'll be doing.

Basic kit. This kit contains sewing tools and notions for hand mending.

Family kit. This kit contains equipment from the basic kit, plus special tools and notions for your most frequent repairs.

Sewing-machine-plus kit. The totally equipped clothing repair kit includes items from the basic and family kits plus a sewing machine and accessories.

Basic Kit

Whether off at college or setting up your first home or apartment, you may not have a sewing machine, so most of your mending will probably be done by hand. You can organize a few basic sewing tools in a small sewing basket, decorative tin or fishing tackle box. For this basic kit, use a hand-held button sewer instead of a sewing machine to quickly tack and repair seams and hems.

Hand needles. For general sewing, use *sharps*, medium-length needles with small round eyes and sharp points. Keep a package of assorted sizes (3/9) on hand. Use *crewel/embroidery needles* with large eyes for easy threading.

Pins. Size 17 stainless steel dressmaker pins will not rust and are an all-purpose size. Pins with plastic heads are comfortable on fingers and easy to see in bulky fabric or when dropped on the floor. Throw away pins that become dull with use because they can damage or snag fabric. Keep pins in a handy pin cushion.

Safety pins. Although safety pins should not be used for permanent repairs, they are critical for emergency mending. Keep an assortment of sizes in your mending kit.

Thread. Five basic colors of thread will cover most mending needs. Choose an all-purpose dark thread (black, brown or navy) that matches your basic wardrobe color. Add spools of white, red, and a medium shade of gray or tan. Complete the assortment with transparent monofilament thread which can be used with any color of fabric.

Thimble. Wear a thimble on your middle finger while hand sewing. Thimbles are available in sizes 6 (small) to 12 (large) and should fit snugly.

Needle threader. This flexible wire loop slips through the eye of a needle to ease threading of

hand and machine needles. It is also a handy tool for pulling knit snags to the wrong side.

Seam ripper. This tool makes it easy to cut seams open, rip hems and remove stitching. Use the pointed end for removing cut threads.

Scissors. Good quality 6" (15 cm) scissors with one sharp point are essential for clipping, snipping and trimming. Use these scissors only for sewing so the blades stay sharp.

Seam gauge. Use a 6" (15 cm) seam gauge with a sliding marker for making small measurements, such as hems and button locations.

Glue stick. Instead of pinning or basting, use a glue stick to provide a temporary bond for hems, trims, appliques and zippers.

Liquid fray preventer. This colorless plastic liquid controls fraying and raveling by stiffening yarns along a cut edge of fabrics. Also use it on buttonholes that become ragged and to control runs in pantyhose.

Beeswax or white candle stub. Before hand sewing, pull thread across one of these waxy substances to reduce knotting and tangling.

Extra buttons. Keep a small container of buttons in basic styles and colors to replace lost and broken buttons. You may want to store extra buttons that often come with coats, dresses, jackets and blouses in this container so you will not forget where they are.

Hooks, eyes and snaps. Have on hand assorted sizes in nickel and black finish for light and dark fabrics.

Button sewer. This hand-held appliance speeds sewing on flat buttons. It can also be used for tacking seams and hems.

Family Kit

This kit contains equipment from the basic kit, plus special tools and notions for your most frequent repairs. To make mending tasks easy, use iron-on patches and appliques, hand-held mending appliances and a portable mending machine to take the place of a sewing machine.

Trimming shears. Use shears instead of scissors for cutting excess fabric from hems and seams. Shears have longer blades and one handle is larger than the other to make cutting more comfortable.

Tape measure. Use a 60" (152 cm) flexible cloth or plastic tape for body and garment measurements.

Yardstick or skirt marker. A skirt marker is a ruler that stands upright on a base. A sliding marker can be positioned the desired distance from the floor to ensure even hems.

Liquid marking pencil. Felt-tip pens for marking the placement of trims, hems and alterations are available in two types. One type leaves a mark that fades and disappears within a few hours; the other rinses off easily with water.

Fusible web, iron-on patches and appliques. Fusible web is a nonwoven bonding agent available in strips and sheets. Place it between two layers of fabric, then press with an iron to melt the web and bond the layers. Iron-on patches are available in basic colors. Use precut iron-on shapes, or purchase larger pieces to be cut to desired size. Iron-on appliques

are an instant way to cover holes and tears in children's clothing.

Steam/dry iron. Fusible and iron-on mending materials make the iron a valuable mending aid. Because most fusible and iron-on interfacings require moisture to bond, keep a press cloth and/or spray bottle of water handy when mending with one of these products.

Press cloth. Use a lint-free press cloth when adhering fusible interfacings and when pressing on the right side of a garment.

Iron soleplate cover. This plate attaches to the soleplate of any iron to prevent scorching and shine on fabrics. It allows you to iron fabrics at a high temperature without a press cloth; fusible and iron-on mending tapes will not stick to it.

Table-top ironing board. Use this ironing board on a table or countertop for small pressing jobs.

Portable mending machine. This small machine uses a straight stitch to sew patches, hems and seams.

Hem-and-seam tacker. This portable appliance quickly tacks hems and seams with tiny, secure stitches. Also use it to tack bows in place and anchor zipper tapes that are starting to rip out.

Hole-and-tear mender. This hand-held mending appliance uses low heat and a special fusing agent to invisibly mend holes in wool, cotton and synthetics.

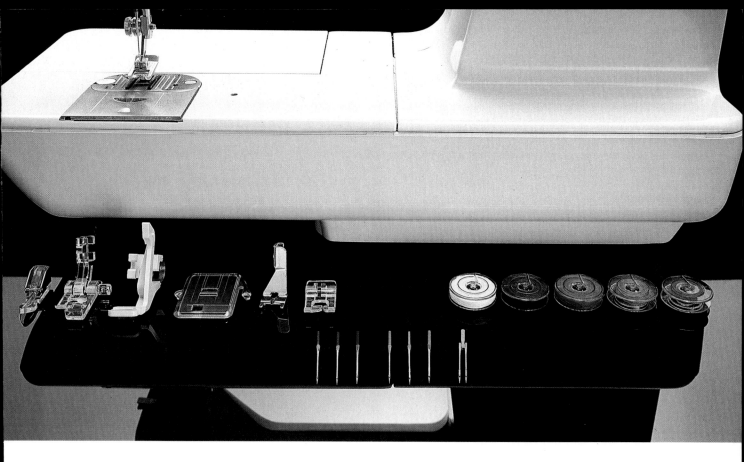

Sewing-Machine-Plus Kit

The totally equipped clothing repair kit includes items from the basic and family kits plus a sewing machine and accessories. Repair clothing with the machine whenever possible to save time and achieve sturdier, better-looking results. For convenience, keep sewing equipment and notions in two containers, one with items you will need at the machine and a mini-basket to take to a comfortable chair for hand sewing.

Sewing machine. A basic *straight-stitch machine* speeds sewing. A *zigzag machine* has other stitch capabilities useful for mending. Zigzag machines may also be equipped with multi-stitch zigzag and special stretch stitches. *Blindstitch hemming* is also available on most zigzag machines. Tubular areas, such as pants legs and sleeve cuffs, are easiest to stitch when using a sewing machine with a *free arm*.

Sewing machine needles. Use ballpoint needles for knit fabrics and regular-point needles for woven fabrics. Keep three sizes on hand: size 11/70 for lightweight fabrics, such as lingerie tricots and sheer wovens; size 14/80 for mediumweight fabrics, such as knits used in T-shirts and sportswear; size 16/90 for heavyweight fabrics, such as bulky knits, denim, and corduroy. Change the needle often because a dull, bent or burred needle can damage fabric. Avoid sewing over pins, which can damage the needle.

Bobbins. To save mending time, wind several bobbins at once with your five basic mending colors. Use the same thread in the needle and bobbin for best results.

Feed cover plate. When darning with a free side-to-side or forward/backward motion, cover or lower the *feed*. (The feed controls the fabric as you sew, moving it forward under the needle.) Check your machine manual to determine if you need a feed cover plate or if your machine has a built-in adjustment for lowering the feed.

Zipper foot. Because the zipper foot adjusts to either side of the needle, you can sew an even line of stitching close to each side of the zipper. Use this foot to stitch cording and piping, or to sew any seam that is bulkier on one side than the other.

Blindstitch hem foot or guide. Some machines have a special foot; others have a hem guide to use with the general-purpose foot.

Darning and embroidery foot. Some machines have a special foot for darning. It allows you to gently pull and push the fabric to achieve long and short stitches. Use with a feed cover plate or lowered feed.

Button foot. When machine-sewing flat buttons, use this foot to hold the button in position. Attaching buttons with the machine can save a great deal of time, especially when sewing several buttons at once.

Special-purpose foot. Use for general-purpose sewing and special tasks such as satin stitching and machine embroidery. A groove under the foot allows for a buildup of thread.

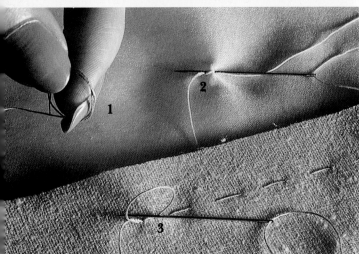

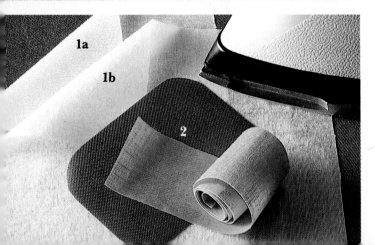

Repair Terms & Techniques

The following six terms describe familiar procedures that appear repeatedly throughout this section. Each general procedure can be done several ways, depending on the type of repair; methods include sewing and non-sewing techniques. When choosing a technique, consider the fabric, available time and equipment, and use of the garment to be repaired.

Baste

1) Hand-baste. Using single thread, take evenly spaced ¼" (6 mm) straight stitches on stitching line.

2) Pin-baste. Place pins at right angles to stitching line so they can be removed easily during sewing.

3) Machine-baste. Use longest stitch on machine, usually 6 to 8 stitches per inch (2.5 cm).

4) Basting tape. Place double-faced basting tape on one layer of fabric close to stitching line. Remove paper covering and place second layer of fabric in position. Do not stitch through tape because it leaves a gummy residue on needle. Remove tape after stitching if it is not water soluble.

5) Glue stick. This water-soluble adhesive forms a temporary bond. Use it sparingly to position trims, pockets and patches. It may also be used on fabrics such as vinyl, where a pin or needle hole would show.

Secure

1) Knot. For single strand, twist end of thread over index finger to form a knot. This knot is easy to remove from start of hand basting.

2) Backstitch. Fasten permanent stitching with a short stitch behind starting point. When you do not want a knot to show on right side of fabric, take two small stitches in same position.

3) Ending knot. Take two small backstitches, inserting needle through second stitch to form loop. Pull thread taut to knot.

Fuse

1) Fusible interfacings. Use **(a)** woven or **(b)** knit. These are applied with heat and steam. Follow instructions on wrapper.

2) Iron-on mending fabrics. These heavy, adhesive-backed fabrics are available as precut patches, tapes and appliques. They usually adhere with a lower heat than interfacings and without steam. Before applying, test iron-on products on an inconspicuous area of the garment; they may make the fabric too stiff.

Reinforce

1) Fusibles. Fusible interfacing or mending fabric provides extra strength to fabric that is wearing thin.

2) Two rows of stitching. Use normal stitch length with second row of stitching in seam allowance ⅛" (3 mm) from the first.

3) Stretch stitches. These built-in machine stitches usually use a forward/backward motion, putting more thread into a seam to provide "give." They are not restricted to stretch and knit fabrics.

4) Fabric. Stitch ½" (1.3 cm) wide twill tape or lightweight fabric into a straight or curved seam.

5) Small stitches. Use stitch length of 18 to 20 stitches per inch (2.5 cm) to stitch stress seams or areas to be clipped.

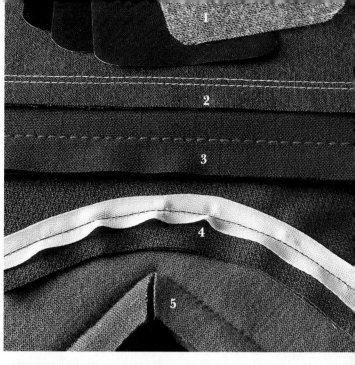

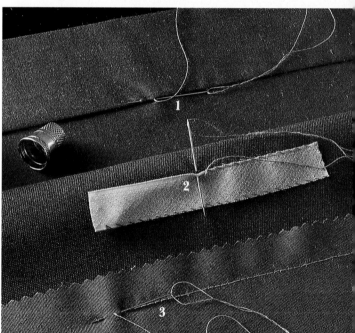

Hand-stitch

1) Slipstitch. Use to join two edges when a nearly invisible stitch is desired. One edge must be on a fold. Working from right to left, slip needle through fold for about ¼" (6 mm). Then take a stitch directly opposite fold, catching only one or two threads. Continue stitching alternating between fold and edge of fabric.

2) Whipstitch. Use to permanently hold two edges of fabric together. Insert needle at right angle to edge, picking up only a few threads. Stitch is slanted. Place stitches as close together as necessary.

3) Backstitch. This strong hand stitch duplicates machine stitching. Take small stitches, working from right to left, inserting needle behind previous stitch. Bring needle up same distance in front of stitch. Continue to insert and bring up needle half a stitch length behind and in front of previous stitch.

Machine-stitch

1) Normal straight stitch. Use 10 to 12 stitches per inch (2.5 cm).

2) Zigzag stitch. For most zigzag stitching, use full *width*. This is usually the highest number on the machine. Stitch *length* adjustment determines whether the stitch is widely or closely spaced.

3) Multi-stitch zigzag. This stitch places three short stitches in the width of one zigzag stitch.

4) Stretch stitches. If your machine has stretch stitches, they may be **(a)** forward/backward straight stitches, **(b)** a combination of straight and zigzag stitches, or **(c)** decorative stitching that combines straight and zigzag stitches, such as honeycomb.

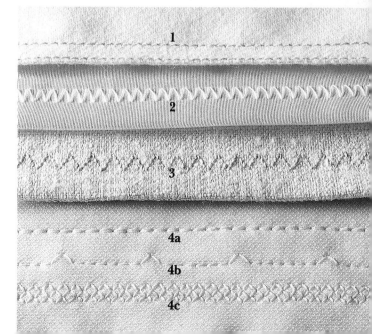

Buttons

A button that is sewn on securely and correctly should last the life of the garment. Prevent the loss of a loose button by resewing it as soon as you notice threads are starting to fray. One loose button often means that others are about to fall off too, so check all the buttons when you resew one.

If a button is lost and you cannot find a perfect match, rearrange the buttons on the garment. Place the unmatching button near the hem or on a pocket or cuff, where it will be less conspicuous.

It may be necessary to replace all the buttons on a garment if a missing one cannot be matched. Select buttons the same size and type as the original to be sure they will fit the buttonholes.

Except for buttons that can be sewn flat on shirts, blouses and other lightweight fabrics, all buttons should be sewn on with a shank. A shank raises the button slightly away from the garment to allow for the thickness of the buttonhole. Make a thread shank for sew-through buttons. On shank buttons, the shank is a part of the button, so it does not usually need a thread shank.

For a buttonhole to lie smoothly when the garment is closed, the shank should be ⅛" (3 mm) longer than the thickness of the fabric. It should be long, almost floppy, on coats and bulky outerwear.

Use buttonhole twist/topstitching, silk or all-purpose thread, six-strand embroidery floss, waxed dental floss or elastic thread to attach buttons by hand. Use a crewel needle with a large eye for easy threading when using buttonhole twist, floss or elastic thread. Match the color of the thread to the color of the button.

To save time, use four strands of thread. Fold thread in half; insert folded end through crewel needle. Knot cut ends and folded end together. Sew on a button with only two stitches through each hole.

All hand-sewn buttons. Cut thread 30" (76 cm) long and run it over beeswax or white candle stub to prevent tangling. Fold thread in half and insert folded end in needle. Knot cut ends together. Insert needle on right side of garment at button position. Take several small stitches in place to secure thread. Cut off knot.

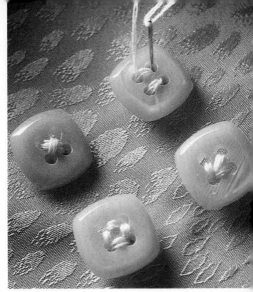

Flat buttons. Secure thread and slide button onto needle. Position button to match other buttons on garment. With needle straight up and down, stitch loosely through each hole several times. Four-hole buttons may be sewn with stitches that cross in center, form a square or parallel lines, or radiate from one hole.

Elastic thread. Use for buttons under strain, such as the bottom button on coatdress. Thread a crewel needle with a single strand of elastic thread. Do not knot. Secure thread with short stitches. Sew on button as for button with thread shank, using only two or three stitches through each hole.

Metal buttons. These buttons have a tendency to cut thread, so use the round eye of a hook and eye set for extra strength. Thread the eye through the metal shank of button. Secure thread. Sew the eye in place through two holes. The button wears against the metal eye, not the thread.

Buttons with thread shank. Secure thread, position button and take a loose stitch through each hole. Insert toothpick between thread and button. Take three or four stitches through each hole. Bring needle to right side of garment, under button. Remove toothpick and wind thread around stitches to form shank. Take several small stitches through shank to secure.

Buttons with extra long shank. Secure thread, position button and place fabric over index finger. With thumb, hold button against fabric but well away from the garment. Take several stitches through each hole. Bring needle to right side of garment under button. Lift button and work blanket stitch around stitches to form thread shank. Secure thread under button.

Shank buttons. Secure thread. Sew shank to garment with several stitches through shank and fabric. Secure thread with two small stitches under shank. If fabric is thick and needs additional shank, insert toothpick between shank and fabric and sew as for button with thread shank.

Reinforce buttons on fragile fabrics, raincoats, jackets and coats to prevent tearing of fabric. Place a small, flat button inside garment, directly under fashion button. Sew through both buttons at the same time. Insert toothpick. Make shank and secure as for button with thread shank.

Sewing machine may be used to attach buttons on light to mediumweight fabrics. Attach button foot and feed cover plate (or drop the feed). Tape or glue button in place. Center button under foot and lower presser foot. Turn handwheel to adjust stitch width to holes in button. Check manual for specific instructions.

Button sewer attaches buttons quickly and easily. Insert garment under clamp and place button under holder. Squeeze and release hand-lever seven or eight times. For four-hole buttons, adjust dial and repeat for other set of holes. Machine has a setting to cut thread when finished.

Snaps & Other Fasteners

Fasteners may have to be replaced when they are not strong enough for the position on the garment or there is too much stress on the area. If the fastener is not strong enough, replace it with a sturdier closure. If the garment is too tight, it may be possible to move the fastener over slightly.

Snaps should be used only where there is little strain on the closure. A snap that does not stay closed can be replaced with a larger, heavy-duty snap or with hook and loop tape, such as Velcro®.

Heavy-duty snaps can replace ordinary snaps or overlapping hooks and eyes on sturdy, heavyweight fabrics, children's clothes and work clothes. These snaps are available in colors and a variety of metal finishes. Apply with special snap pliers or a hammer and small tool as specified on the package.

Hooks and eyes are usually used on waistbands or above zippers where they are inconspicuous. If the finished edges just meet, use a hook with a round eye; if the edges overlap, use a hook with a straight eye. Use two sets for strength on a waistband.

Heavy-duty hooks and eyes are used on waistbands as a sturdier closure than ordinary hooks and eyes. These hooks are strong and flat so they will not slide out of the eye.

Hook and loop tape can be used where two edges overlap, such as at waistbands or center front openings. It is available in three weights and in three shapes. Sew hook and loop closures in place by hand or machine, or use a special adhesive to secure them to vinyl and other hard-surfaced fabrics. Hook and loop closures are an excellent replacement for ordinary snaps or hooks and eyes on clothing for children or handicapped persons.

How to Attach Hooks and Eyes

Hooks and eyes. Sew hook on underside of overlap without stitching through to right side. Using single strand of waxed thread, take four or five stitches through each hole. Take two or three stitches across the end, under the hook, to hold it flat. Position eye in place and tack through holes as for hook. Secure thread on underside.

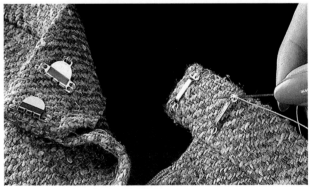

Heavy-duty waistband hooks and eyes. Attach as for hook and eye application. For extra strength and security, use two sets on waistbands of pants and skirts. Place one directly above the zipper and the other at end of underlap.

How to Attach Snaps

Snaps. Attach ball section to overlap and socket section to underlap. Using single strand of waxed thread, secure thread at snap location. Take three or four straight stitches up through each hole; do not stitch through to right side of garment. Secure thread with tiny stitches in fabric at last hole.

Heavy-duty snaps. Each side of heavy-duty snap is in two sections, applied with a special tool. Follow instructions on package. Because of their weight, snaps must be used with at least two thicknesses of fabric reinforced with interfacing.

How to Attach Hook and Loop Tape

Machine-stitch hook side (stiff and scratchy) on underlap and loop side (softer) on overlap. Sew circles in the shape of a triangle; stitch strips and squares on all four sides. You will want this as neat as possible when stitching shows on right side.

Hand-sew with single strand of waxed thread. Whipstitch edges, being careful not to go through to right side of overlap. When stitching underlap, which will not show on right side, stitch through all layers of fabric.

Replace buttons and buttonholes with hook and loop tape if desired. Hand-sew the buttonhole closed with short whipstitches. Stitch square or circle of loop side of tape behind buttonhole. Stitch hook side of tape on button location. Sew a non-functional button on buttonhole.

Sew hook and loop tape on waistband, using strip of tape. Stitch hook side to underlap and loop side to overlap, stitching on all four sides. Waistband is adjustable in garments without a zipper, such as wrap-around skirts.

Split Seams

Repairing a split seam is one of the most common mending tasks. The simplest remedy is to repair with machine straight stitching. This solution, however, may not be sufficient in the long run. Analyze the cause of the seam failure and choose a method of repair that will strengthen the seam.

Thread in seams may wear out and break before the rest of the garment, particularly if the thread is all-cotton and the fabric is long-wearing polyester. Check the fiber label and use thread with the same fiber content whenever possible. Seams in knit or actionwear garments often split because they were sewn with thread that was not strong enough to "give" with the natural stretchiness of the fabric, or a straight stitch was used when a special stretch stitch should have been applied.

Certain seams often wear out and split before others in a garment. These are the *stress seams*, and include seams in the crotch, underarm and pockets. If you sew your own clothing, these seams should be reinforced in the construction as a preventive measure. When these seams split in purchased garments, repair them with smaller stitches, two rows of stitching or machine reinforcement stitching.

Split seams may indicate the garment is too tight and too much stress is being placed on the seam. This situation may result in a *pulled seam* in which the fabric pulls away from an intact seam. The seam may need reinforcing or may have to be let out a bit to add extra space.

Seams in knits and sweaters are apt to rip at the ends because they were not secured with a lockstitch. Replace these seams with hand backstitching or machine stretch stitch.

How to Repair Split Seams

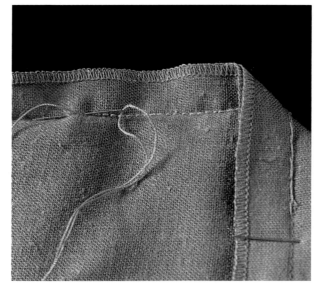

Machine-stitched seams. Remove loose threads at each end of broken seam. Using thread appropriate to fabric, start stitching in seam allowance 1" (2.5 cm) from end of split seam; taper to original seamline. Overlap stitching ½" (1.3 cm) at each end of broken seam; stitch back into seam allowance. It may be necessary to finish some seams by hand if the area is awkward to reach with the machine, for instance where underarm and armhole seams meet.

Hand-stitched seams. Using short needle and single thread, secure thread ½" (1.3 cm) from end of broken thread. To backstitch, insert needle ⅛" (3 mm) behind point where the thread came out. Bring needle forward and out the same distance in front of the point. Continue to insert and bring up needle half a stitch length behind and in front of previous stitch. Stitches on underside are twice as long as on right side; stitch looks like machine stitching on right side.

How to Reinforce Stress Seams

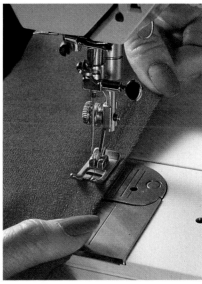

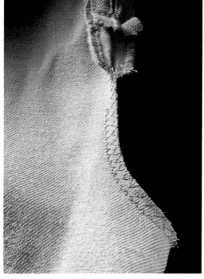

Knit seams. Reinforce knit seams by stretching seam slightly as you sew to incorporate more thread and "give" into the seam. Sew one row on original seamline, then another row ⅛" (3 mm) inside seam allowance. If machine has stretch stitches, use forward/backward or special knit stitch.

Crotch and armhole seams. Zigzag with narrow stitch on seamline. Because stitch length is short and width is narrow, extra thread enables seam to stretch slightly without ripping. On straight-stitch machine, stitch two rows, one on original seamline and second ⅛" (3 mm) inside. Use short stitches, 18 to 20 per inch (2.5 cm).

Actionwear seams. With zigzag machine, stitch on seamline with special built-in stretch stitches or narrow zigzag. Trim seam allowances to ¼" (6 mm); sew together with zigzag or multi-stitch zigzag. With straight-stitch machine, stitch two rows close together and a third row in the seam allowance ¼" (6 mm) from the first two.

How to Repair a Pulled Seam (fused method)

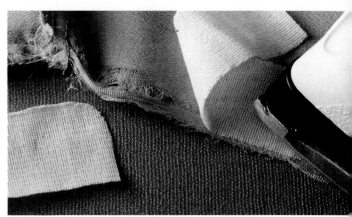

1) Remove stitching from pulled area and 1" (2.5 cm) beyond each end of pulled seam. Under stress, seams in silky and loosely woven fabrics may pull, distorting fabric but leaving seam stitching intact.

2) Cut two strips of soft, lightweight iron-on interfacing (such as fusibile knit) 1" (2.5 cm) wide and as long as opening. Round corners. Fuse interfacing on wrong sides of both seam allowances.

How to Repair a Pulled Seam (stitched method)

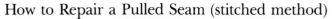

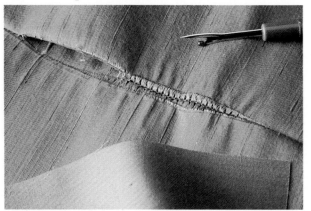

1) Remove stitching from pulled area and 1" (2.5 cm) beyond each end. To replace stitching use thread that matches perfectly because reinforcement stitching may show on right side. Use extra-fine thread for lightweight fabrics.

2) Cut two strips of lightweight fabric for underlay. Place underlay on wrong side of pulled seam allowances. From right side, stitch over loose threads with multi-stitch zigzag, pushing distorted threads together with fingers. Stitch several times.

How to Repair a Seam from Right Side

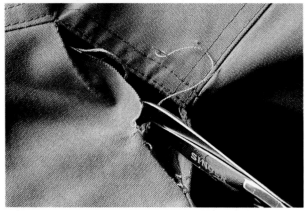

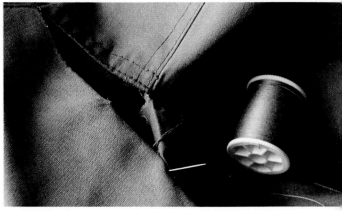

1) Trim loose threads from seam. Armhole seams of lined jackets and coats, and topstitched seams may need to be repaired from right side because they are not accessible from inside.

2) Use single strand of matching all-purpose thread on mediumweight garments. Use buttonhole twist on raincoats and outerwear. From inside, insert needle ½" (1.3 cm) from end of broken stitching.

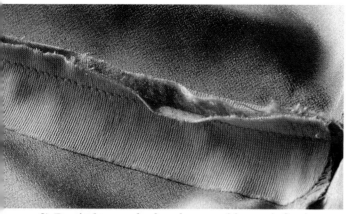

3) Restitch seam by hand or machine, reinforcing with a second row of stitching if necessary.

4) Topstitch the entire length of seam from right side to reinforce.

3) Restitch seam on original seamline; reinforce with short stitches if necessary. On underside, trim underlay close to stitching.

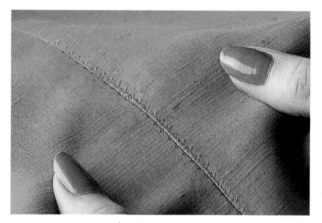

4) Turn to right side. If matching thread is used, repair will not be conspicuous even if zigzag stitching extends into garment.

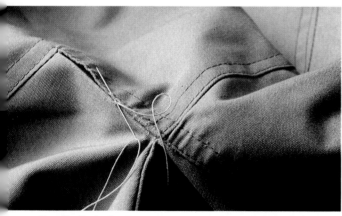

3) Blindstitch along seam. Use tiny stitches, ⅛" to ¼" (3 to 6 mm) long, on each side of seam, pulling edges together. Continue ½" (1.3 cm) beyond split. Secure thread with small stitches in place.

Lining Seams. Whipstitch from right side. Fold edges of seam to inside. Working toward body of garment, insert needle at right angle to folded edges, picking up only one or two threads at a time.

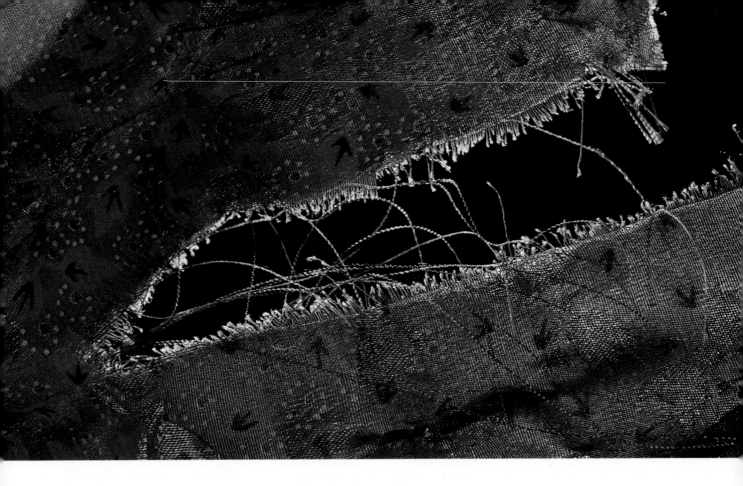

Tears, Cuts & Holes

Rips, tears and cuts are usually the result of an accidental snag on a sharp object. The threads or yarns of a rip or cut are usually not missing as they are in a hole, but they may have been pulled off-grain. Holes leave a gap in fabric with threads missing. What starts as a worn spot or small tear may become a hole, and the longer it is ignored the larger it becomes. Repair it as soon as possible.

Repair without sewing. Use fusible interfacing, iron-on mending tape or fabric, or fusible web with a patch of matching fabric. If a tear has not raveled excessively, the fusible prevents further tearing or raveling. On most fabrics it will barely be noticeable; however, fusibles add stiffness and bulk that may not be desirable on lightweight or sheer fabrics. Before making a repair, test the fusible on a hidden area of the garment, such as in a seam allowance, a shirttail or the inside of a pocket.

Hand darning. Use thread that is suitable to the weight of the fabric. Thread that is too heavy strains the darned area and makes the mend more obvious; thread that is too fine may not cover the hole adequately. To match woven fabrics perfectly, ravel some threads from a seam or cut edge to use for hand darning. Steam press to remove the crimp.

Machine darning. Some machines have a special darning foot to use with a free-hand straight stitch.

For straight-stitch darning, drop or cover the feed. To manipulate the area to be darned more easily, place it in an embroidery hoop.

Machine darning may be done with or without an underlay of lightweight or matching fabric. If the tear is so large that the trimmed edges of the fabric do not meet smoothly, an underlay gives strength and support to it without excessive stitching. This is a sturdy mend, ideal for fabrics that receive a lot of stress or require frequent laundering. To make this mend less obvious, use thread one shade darker than the fabric. Use extra-fine thread for light to mediumweight fabrics.

When darning denim jeans, use matching navy thread on top and gray thread in the bobbin. Loosen upper tension. The bobbin thread will pull slightly to the top of the work, giving an almost invisible mend.

Use multi-stitch zigzag, serpentine or honeycomb stitch for darning and reinforcement with zigzag machines. These stitches keep the fabric flat and allow the mended area to stretch slightly after it has been repaired.

Sometimes a tear is hidden, such as in a gathered area. If a tiny tuck will not affect the fit of the garment, the tear can be mended on the inside with a narrow seam.

How to Repair a Tear or Cut without Sewing

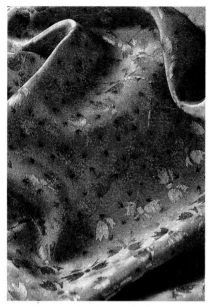

1) Press torn area to realign threads which may have been pulled off-grain. Trim loose threads from edges of tear with sharp scissors. Clip into each end about ½" (1.3 cm), or enough to taper to a point.

2) Place tear, face down, on pressing surface and gently bring edges together. Cut patch of fusible interfacing or mending fabric 1" (2.5 cm) larger than tear. Round corners. Place patch, adhesive side down, over tear. Touch tip of iron to patch to tack in place.

3) Turn garment right side up. Check that cut edges meet, covering patch. Press to fuse, following directions on package. Let cool before handling.

How to Hand-darn a Tear or Cut

1) Prepare tear as in step 1, above. Use fishbone stitch to hold torn edges together. Use matching thread because it may be impossible to remove. Do not secure thread. Insert needle ¼" (6 mm) from end of tear, then on one side of tear at end.

2) Alternate slanted stitches on each side of tear with needle in position as at left; alternate direction of needle with each stitch. Place stitches ⅛" to ¼" (3 to 6 mm) apart. Insert needle as close to torn edge as possible.

3) Stitch back and forth across tear with closely spaced rows of tiny running stitches. Work parallel to fabric grain, duplicating weave of fabric. Keep stitches loose so darned area does not have tight, pulled appearance. (Contrasting thread is used for detail.)

How to Machine-darn a Tear or Cut

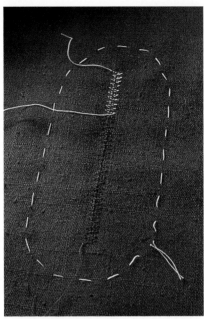

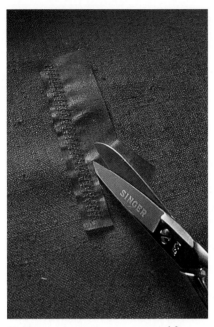

1) Follow step 1 for repairing a tear (page 67). Cut a patch of lightweight fabric in matching color, 3" (7.5 cm) larger than tear. Baste it in position on back of tear.

2) Multi-stitch zigzag, serpentine or honeycomb stitch on right side of garment, catching both edges of tear in stitching. (Contrasting thread is used for detail.)

3) Turn garment to wrong side; trim underlay patch close to stitching. If fabric ravels or frays easily, stitch again on each side of first row before trimming, overlapping stitches slightly.

How to Machine-darn a Hole or Reinforce a Worn Area

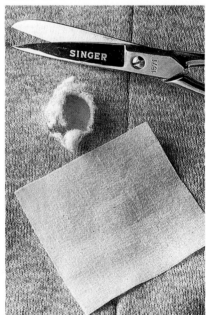

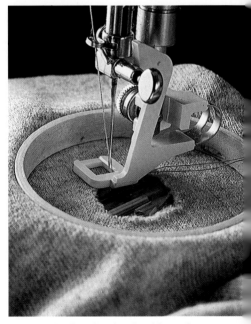

1) Trim ragged thread ends from hole. If using an underlay for reinforcement, cut a patch of lightweight woven fabric at least 1" (2.5 cm) larger than hole or worn area. Baste underlay on wrong side, covering area to be darned.

2) Place area to be darned in embroidery hoop, right side up over outer ring. Place smaller ring inside outer ring so area to be darned will lie flat on machine. Pull fabric taut in hoop.

3) Attach darning/embroidery foot and feed cover (or lower feed). Raise needle to highest position; carefully position hoop under needle. Lower presser foot lever. Insert needle into fabric. Bring bobbin thread up through fabric and pull threads behind needle.

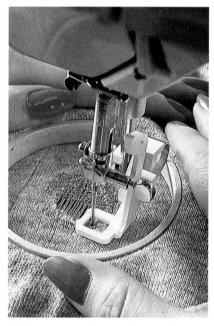

4) Stitch a circle around hole, holding hoop with both hands. Stitch slowly; do not rotate hoop. Clip thread ends. Move hoop slowly back and forth under needle to fill in with vertical stitches. Control stitch length by hand movements.

5) Move work from side to side under needle after vertical threads have been stitched. Continue stitching until hole is filled in with vertical and horizontal stitches.

Reinforce a worn area or darn a hole with multi-stitch zigzag, serpentine or honeycomb stitch. Place underlay under worn area. Stitch back and forth over worn area, overlapping stitches.

Patches

Whether a repair is invisible or decorative, patching is a sturdy way to repair holes in garments. A favorite skirt with a tear that is inconspicuously patched may remain in your wardrobe instead of being discarded. A child's worn snowsuit mended with decorative knee patches can start the season with a new look.

Methods of patching include fusing, gluing, and hand or machine stitching. The patching technique you choose depends on how much time you have, the use of the garment and the type of fabric.

Time. Fusing a patch usually takes the least amount of time, especially if you buy a precut, iron-on patch. Other time-saving notions include mending fabric or tape and fusible web. Use a hole-and-tear mending appliance to repair small holes and tears, such as those from cigarette burns and moths. For successful application, follow package or wrapper directions when using any fusible or iron-on product.

Applying fabric glue or adhesive is another simple way to patch when stitching is too obvious and fusing is not possible. Special adhesive products are available for vinyl, leather and nylon outerwear.

Machine-stitch a patch for a fast, secure repair that will withstand frequent laundering. With this method you can use decorative stitch patterns around the edge of the patch. Use a free-arm sewing machine to machine-stitch patches on sleeves or pants legs.

Hand stitching is the most time-consuming method of patching, but may need to be used in an area that is hard to reach with a machine. The patch can be applied so that it is nearly invisible on carefully matched plaids.

Use. Another consideration, besides the amount of time a patching technique takes, is the use of the garment. Expensive dressy clothes require less obvious patching than rugged work clothes or children's play clothes. A fused patch of matching fabric is the best technique to use for a good pair of gabardine pants, but a sturdy machine-stitched patch would be appropriate for jeans. Machine or hand stitching may be best for children's clothes whenever fusing or gluing would cause the fabric to become uncomfortably stiff.

Fabric. Consider, too, the type of fabric. Tweeds, plaids and overall prints are easier to repair invisibly than fabrics of solid colors. Textured fabrics are easier to patch than smooth ones. Solid colors, smooth surfaces and lightweight fabrics may require lace or applique trims to cover the repaired area.

To cover a hole least conspicuously, use a patch that matches the fabric of the garment. Save scrap material from clothing you have sewn. If the garment was purchased, cut a small patch from the hem, the back of a pocket or another concealed area of the garment. Apply the patch *under* the hole for a hidden application. Apply it *over* the hole and stitch around the edge for a decorative application.

Repairing with Fusible and Iron-on Patches

Apply purchased iron-on patch that is compatible with fiber, color and texture of garment. Wash or dryclean garment before applying patch. Preheat worn area with dry iron before applying patch.

Cut mending fabric or tape 1" (2.5 cm) larger than hole or tear; round off corners. Place shiny side of mending patch on right side of garment, covering hole. Use press cloth to prevent scorching.

Use fusible web to make an iron-on patch from any fabric. Cut fabric patch and web 1" (2.5 cm) larger than hole. Place web between fabric patch and hole. Adhere, using steam iron.

Fuse and reinforce with stitching to keep edge smooth and secure on garments that need frequent laundering. Use straight, zigzag or decorative stitch.

Use preventive fusing to reinforce areas that receive hard wear, such as elbows. Back with fusible interfacing, cut wide enough to stitch into seams.

How to Use Hole-and-Tear Mending Appliance

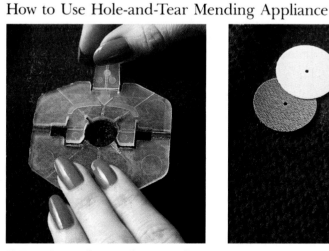

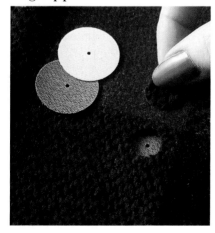

1) Punch out damaged area and patch, using fabric clamp.

2) Place bonding circle under hole; position patch, matching grainlines.

3) Bond patch with backing material and low-heat appliance.

71

How to Hand-stitch a Patch

1) Press fabric around hole. Trim hole to square or rectangle. Reinforce corners with short machine stitches, or small running stitches ¼" (6 mm) from edge. Clip corners up to stitching. Reinforce corners with liquid fray preventer.

2) Turn edges under ¼" (6 mm) and press. Cut patch on matching grain 1½" (3.8 cm) larger than hole. With right sides up, center patch under hole. Baste in place along folded edge.

How to Machine-stitch a Patch on the Inside

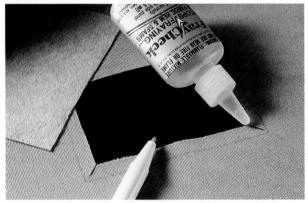

1) Press fabric around hole. Trim hole to square or rectangle. On wrong side, mark ¼" (6 mm) seam along edge of hole or reinforce as in step 1, above. Clip to marks at corners. Reinforce corners with liquid fray preventer. Cut matching fabric patch 1" (2.5 cm) larger than hole.

2) Press edges of hole under ¼" (6 mm). With right sides together, line up one edge of patch with edge of hole, opening out pressed seam allowance. Work from wrong side of garment. Using short stitches, stitch ¼" (6 mm) from edge, starting at middle of one side. Stitch to corner.

How to Patch with Fabric Glue or Adhesive

1) Trim hole or tear to a simple shape with smooth edges. Cut a patch of matching fabric the exact same size and shape as hole. Cut underlay of lightweight matching fabric at least 1" (2.5 cm) larger than patch.

2) Apply a narrow bead of permanent fabric glue to edge on wrong side of patch; use toothpick or pin to spread. Press patch onto underlay fabric and allow to dry thoroughly.

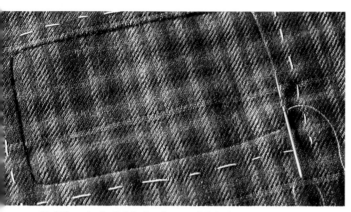

3) Slipstitch folded edges of fabric to patch, using tiny, closely spaced stitches, ⅛" to ¼" (3 to 6 mm) long. Use a short, fine needle.

4) Catchstitch edge of patch to garment on inside, picking up only one or two threads of garment so stitches are not visible on outside. On lightweight fabrics, turn under edge of patch and slipstitch.

3) Pivot at corner. To pivot, leave needle in fabric; raise presser foot. Turn patch a quarter turn. Rearrange garment in front of needle, lining up raw edge of hole with patch. Lower presser foot.

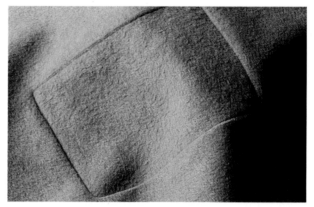

4) Stitch each side of patch, pivoting at each corner. Overlap stitching at starting point. Press patch and seams to one side.

3) Apply glue sparingly to edge of hole. From underneath, place patch right side up into hole. Remove any excess glue with damp cloth.

4) Place tape at right angles to edges until glue is dry. Let dry for a few minutes. Trim underlay close to glue line.

Elbow & Knee Patches

Worn elbow and knee areas do not always need to be invisibly repaired. Instead, apply decorative patches. Appliqued knee patches are ideal for jeans. Synthetic or genuine suedes make handsome elbow patches for sweaters, jackets and wool shirts. You can cut your own, or buy precut suede and leather patches with perforations around the edges to aid in sewing through the heavy patch.

To cut patches, first make a paper or cardboard pattern. For nonwoven fabrics that do not ravel, such as synthetic suede, cut the patch the same size as the pattern. For woven fabrics that ravel, such as corduroy, cut patch ½" (1.3 cm) larger, press edges under ¼" (6 mm).

Baste or fuse patches in place for stitching. To fuse, cut fusible web from pattern. Place fusible web between patch and right side of garment. Place heavy brown paper or aluminum foil under worn area to prevent fusible web from sticking to inside of garment.

How to Apply Elbow and Knee Patches

1) Make a paper or cardboard pattern 4" by 5" (10 by 12.5 cm) for sleeve patch and 5" by 6" (12.5 by 15 cm) for knee patch, depending on size of garment. Trim corners into rounded curves. Cut and fuse patch as above.

2) Machine-stitch edge of patch in place (or hand-stitch). Use medium stitch length with thread and needle appropriate to fabric. Free-arm machine makes it easier to sew patches on sleeves and pants legs.

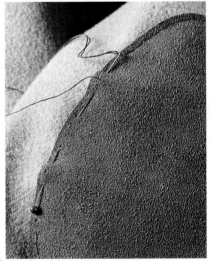

Hand-stitch edge of patch in place. Use backstitch (page 57) or blanket stitch (page 76). Use single strand of buttonhole twist for perforated suede or leather patches and for lined jackets.

How to Applique a Patch on the Outside

1) Press garment area to be patched, but do not trim worn area. Cut matching patch 1" (2.5 cm) larger than area to be patched. With right sides up, center patch over hole or worn area and baste in place.

2) Open part of seam, if necessary, for access to narrow areas. Zigzag around patch, using closely spaced stitches to cover raw edges of patch. Use widest zigzag setting and matching thread.

3) Stitch again using multi-stitch zigzag or decorative stitch to reinforce patch. Use short stitch length and full width. Overlap stitching at corners. Trim worn fabric area from under patch.

Children's Patches

Patches can enhance the appearance and durability of children's clothes. Bright colors and fanciful appliques provide contrast; quilted patches add extra strength and padding for the knees. If only one knee or elbow area wears out, reinforce and patch both pants legs or sleeves for a decorative effect. You will be satisfied knowing the garment will last longer, and children will be delighted with the new look that a patch or applique gives to their clothes.

To coordinate a child's outfit, repeat the fabric or design of the patch on another area of the garment. Trim the pockets, for example, with fabric or a stitch pattern used on the patch. Or coordinate piped patches with piped collar and cuffs on a shirt.

Consider comfort when selecting the patching method you will use. Fusing the patch (page 71) may add too much stiffness to be comfortable. Machine-stitching takes a little longer but is generally softer than fusing.

A free-arm machine aids machine stitching of tubular areas, such as sleeves and pants legs, because you can stitch around the patch all at once. Even with some free-arm machines, you may have to reposition the garment after sewing halfway around the patch and sew from the other end of the tube.

On narrow legs or sleeves, open the inside seam before stitching to provide a flat area. Stitch the patch in place, then restitch the seam. An alternative for hard-to-reach areas is to hand-stitch the patch with backstitch or blanket stitch.

How to Blanket-stitch a Decorative Patch

Use three strands of embroidery floss or a single strand of buttonhole twist. Secure thread under patch. Bring needle to right side. Holding thread loop down with thumb, bring needle through patch and garment and over thread. Pull up stitch. Continue around patch with stitches ⅛" to ⅜" (3 to 10 mm) apart. Secure thread on inside.

How to Apply Padded Knee Patches

1) Cut patch, backing and batting at least 1" (2.5 cm) larger than worn area. Apply any decorative or quilting stitches before sewing patch onto garment. If necessary, edgestitch layers together to prevent shifting.

2) Baste patch onto worn area of garment. Replace presser foot with special-purpose foot for applique work. Set machine for narrow zigzag and medium stitch length. Zigzag around edge of patch.

3) Satin-stitch around edge, completely covering narrow zigzag and edge of patch. To satin-stitch, set machine for wide zigzag and short stitch length; loosen tension. A test sample is advisable.

How to Apply a Quilted Patch with Piped Edges

1) Cut patch with rounded corners. Using zipper foot, stitch piping to right side of patch, beginning 1" (2.5 cm) from end of cord so other end can be lapped around it. Allow 1" (2.5 cm) overlap at ends. Snip a few stitches at overlapped end to open piping. Clip encased cord so ends meet.

2) Fold under ½" (1.3 cm) of overlapped end of piping. Lap it around the other end and stitch in place. Turn seam allowance to wrong side of patch and press raw edges toward center.

3) Baste patch in position and topstitch close to piping, using zipper foot. Stitch a second row approximately ¼" (6 mm) from topstitching.

Creative Repairs with Trimmings

Sometimes the best repair solution is to disguise a tear or hole with lace, ribbon, a pocket, an applique or an insert. If conventional mending techniques would be obvious because of the fabric, or the tear is in a prominent location, turn the repair into a design feature.

Consider the style and fabric of the garment when selecting which trimming to use. Laces, ribbons and ruffles are good choices for little girls' dresses, lingerie and blouses. An applique adds whimsical decoration to children's clothing, even when in an unusual location such as on a sleeve cuff, a dress hem or the seat of pants. A fabric insert is ideal for replacing an area of fabric that would be difficult to trim with another technique or an area that has a large tear in it. Use an insert to replace a yoke, or add a decorative band near the hem of a skirt or inverted pleats in the sleeves of a dress.

Designers use pockets as decorative features in surprising positions. The same idea works as a strategy for repair. Add two or three contrasting pockets, one to hide the tear and the others to call attention to the pocket as a design feature. Not only will the tear be covered, but the garment will have a new look as well.

When selecting trimmings, also consider the garment care and use. Purchased items, such as lace collars or silk flower pins, are also possibilities. For denim or corduroy, sporty appliques or grosgrain ribbons can hide repairs without adding frills.

How to Use Ribbon to Hide Repairs

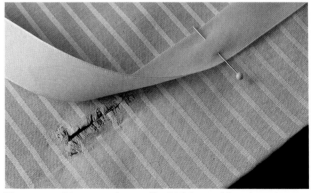

Tears on skirts can be easily hidden with trimmings. Choose a coordinating trimming wide enough to cover the tear. Baste ribbon or lace over the tear and stitch in place. Use liquid fray preventer or fusible interfacing on inside to prevent further raveling. Attach additional trimming at waistband or sleeve to extend the design feature to the whole garment.

How to Use Pockets to Hide Repairs

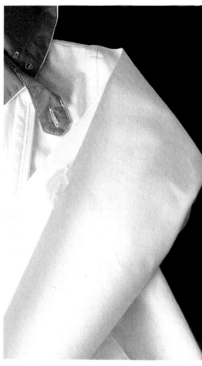

1) Consider the position of the tear when deciding what technique to use. A pocket is a creative way to conceal a tear on a sleeve.

2) Make pockets from contrasting fabrics; add several for emphasis. On a windbreaker, zippered pockets are ideal for a casual look.

3) Coordinate with other pockets on garment. This repair method is especially good for sportswear and children's clothes.

How to Use Fabric Inserts to Hide Repairs

1) Replace torn area with lace or fabric insert if hole or tear is in a position that is not appropriate for trimming.

2) Position lace over hole or tear. Attach with narrow zigzag on finished edge of lace. Trim torn area from behind insert. Use liquid fray preventer on inside cut edges.

3) Use handkerchiefs, embroidered linens or contrasting fabrics for decorative inserts.

Hems

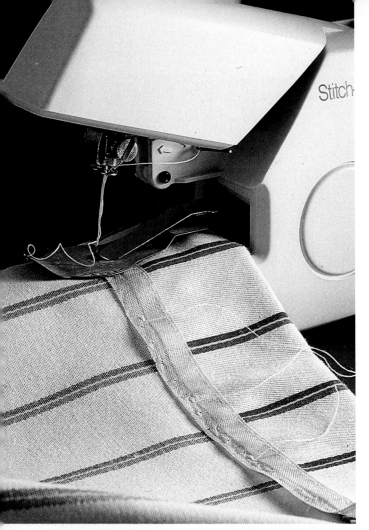

Hem-and-seam tacker makes individual thread tacks, useful for tacking permanent or temporary hems. Place hem under clamp. Squeeze and release hand lever five or six times to stitch. Use built-in thread cutter to automatically cut thread. Make as many tacks as necessary to secure hem in place.

It takes only minutes to repair a hem that has pulled out. Make emergency repairs with double-faced mending tape, fabric glue or a portable hem-and-seam tacker.

Non-sewing repairs can be made with strips of fusible web. This permanent hem withstands washing and drycleaning.

Hand-stitching the repair gives a custom finish. Use blindstitch for woven, ravelly fabrics finished with seam binding or an overcast edge; catchstitch is durable for flat hems in pants, knits and heavy fabrics. Use slipstitch (page 57) for woven fabrics with a turned-under edge.

Machine-stitched repair takes less time and is sturdier than hand stitching, and it achieves the same professional finish. Machine blindstitch provides an invisible hem. A straight-stitched hem shows on the right side.

When in doubt about which hemming or stitching technique to use, duplicate the technique used by the manufacturer in the original hem. Many commercial hems use a blind chainstitch that pulls out when one end of the thread is pulled. Replace this hem with a stitch appropriate to the fabric and the garment use. You may also need to replace poor quality seam binding that has worn from abrasion.

Emergency Repairs

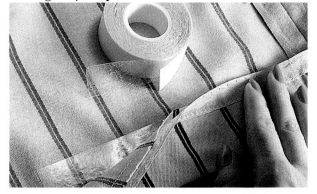

Double-faced mending tape needs no iron to apply. Place tape on garment with edge along hemming line; leave backing on tape. Press firmly with fingers. Remove paper backing. Fold hem up at ends of tape and pinch in place. Smooth hem, applying pressure from center outward. Remove tape before washing or drycleaning.

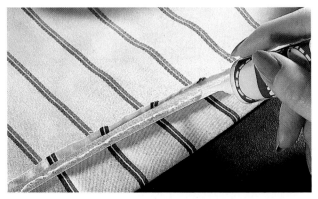

Fabric glue is washable but not drycleanable. Test for staining in a hidden area. Spread foil under fabric to protect work surface. Apply thin line of glue to hem edge. Spread lightly with finger or tube tip. Fold hem in place. Blot excess with damp cloth. Apply light pressure with fingers or use straight pins to hold. Glue dries in five minutes.

Six Ways to Repair a Hem

Fusible web is available by the yard or in precut strips. By the yard it is more economical, but you'll need to cut it into strips ½" to ¾" (1.3 to 2 cm) wide for hemming. Apply web strips between two layers of fabric. Steam press with damp press cloth as directed on package.

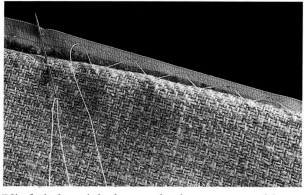

Blindstitch a pinked, overedged or seam-taped hem. Work from right to left. Roll hem edge back about ¼" (6 mm). Take a tiny stitch in the garment. Take next stitch in hem ¼" to ½" (6 mm to 1.3 cm) to left of first stitch. Continue alternating stitches. Keep stitches in garment small and do not pull too tightly.

Replace worn and frayed seam binding on fabrics that ravel. Lap seam binding ¼" (6 mm) over hem edge on right side of fabric. Straight-stitch binding in place, overlapping ends at a seamline. Hem by hand, using blindstitch.

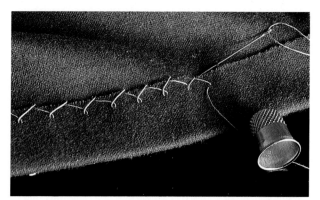

Catchstitch hems on knits and heavy fabrics to provide give, and to hold hem edge flat to garment. Work from left to right. Take a small horizontal stitch in hem edge. Take next stitch in garment, about ¼" (6 mm) to right, crossing the stitches.

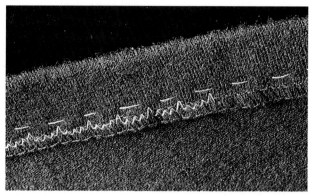

Machine blindstitch for sturdy hems. Baste hem to garment ¼" (6 mm) from raw edge. Adjust machine to blindstitch setting, and attach blindstitch foot or zigzag foot with hemming guide. Place hem face down and fold garment back to basting line. Stitch close to the fold, catching garment only in wide zigzag stitch. Press flat.

Straight-stitch to hem and finish raw edge in one step, or to add decorative detail. Turn up hem 1½" (3.8 cm) and pin in place. For ravelly fabrics, pink or turn under raw edge. On right side, topstitch 1" (2.5 cm) from folded edge. As a design detail, add a second or third row of stitching.

Pants Hems

One of the most frequent tasks of upkeep and repair is hemming. Hems in pants are constantly being snagged and pulled out by shoes. In addition, new pants purchased without hems need to be adjusted to the right length for the wearer.

To determine the correct length for man-tailored pants, try on the pants and pin the hem in position. Allow the pants leg bottom to touch the top of the shoe in front; taper it ¼" (6 mm) longer in the back. The pants leg then brushes the top of the shoe in front without wrinkling, and partially covers the shoe in back.

Measure the other pants leg in the same manner. Or lay pants out flat, one leg on top of the other and mark second leg at the same length.

How to Hem Pants

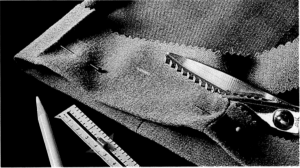

1) Pin hem up to desired length. Press fold lightly without pressing over pins. Trim hem depth to 1½" (3.8 cm). Check to see that hem lies flat.

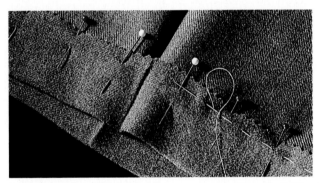

2) Finish raw edge with zigzag or overedge stitch if hem has been trimmed to a new length. For firmly woven fabrics, pink the edge. Baste hem in place ¼" (6 mm) from finished edge.

3) Clip hem deep enough at center front to spread hem to fit inside pants leg. Clip will be from ¼" to ¾" (6 mm to 2 cm) long.

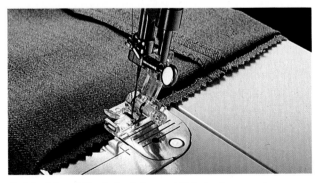

4) Machine-blindstitch hem. This is the most secure hem because stitches are hidden between hem and pants. Use free arm of machine if available. To hand-stitch, use catchstitch.

Vent & Lining Hems

A loose or damaged lining may not be visible to others but can get out of hand if not repaired. If a vent is torn, it is likely the lining needs repair, too. To repair a lining, release the stitching at the hem to reach the area that needs reinforcing or patching.

Repair a pulled hem in a lining with a slipstitch or blindstitch, being sure there is at least an extra ½" (1.3 cm) for ease when folding the lining hem under. Without generous ease at the hemline, the lining will strain and eventually tear or pull loose again.

How to Repair Linings At Vents

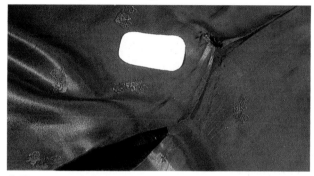

1) Remove stitches of lining at vent and nearby hem. If only lining is torn, fuse a patch of lightweight fabric under tear and reinforce. If garment is torn, patch and repair as for pulled seams (page 64).

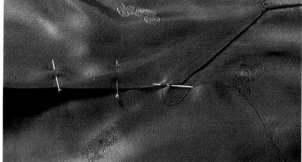

2) Restitch vent and lining on original stitching lines. To reinforce or conceal mended area, follow directions for repairing torn slits, step 2 below.

How to Repair Lining Hems

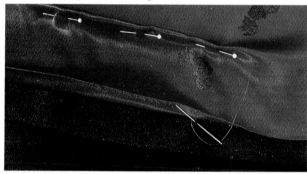

1) Secure loose ends of torn hemming in lining. Pin up ease in lining approximately 2" (5 cm) above lining hem to keep it out of the way when stitching.

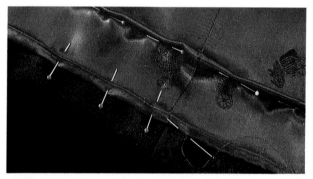

2) Pin lining hem to garment. Blindstitch or slipstitch lining to hem, catching only underlayer of lining. Remove pins and allow ease to cover hem.

How to Repair Torn Slits

Tack torn seam on inside with hem-and-seam tacker to prevent further ripping. On right side of garment, tack across seam at bottom of seamline, catching both sides of seam in tack.

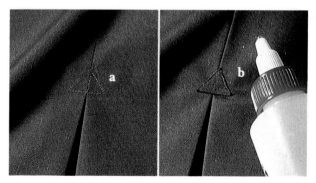

Stitch a triangle reinforcement **(a)** at top of slit, using short straight stitch. Or **(b)** hold in place with a drop of fabric glue and machine-stitch or whipstitch a purchased embroidered arrowhead at top of slit.

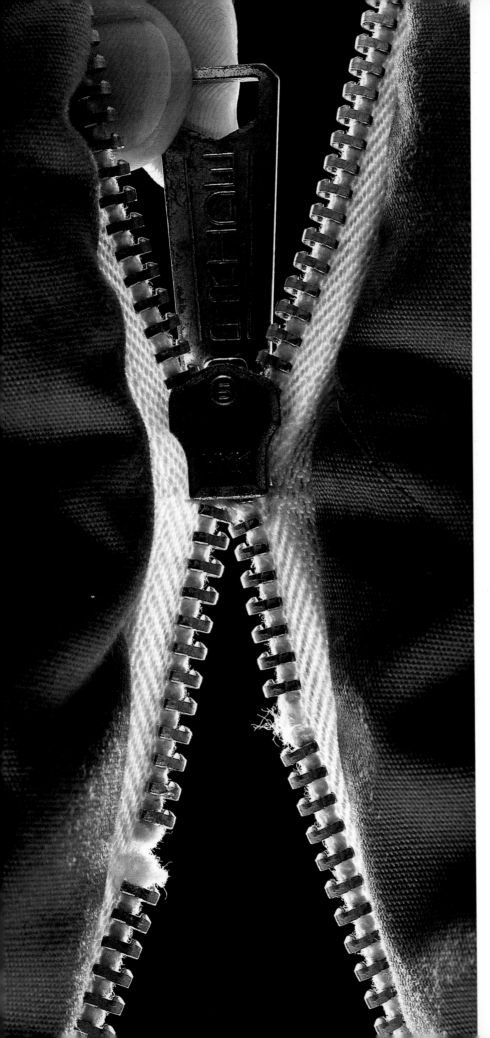

Zippers

Knowing how to replace a broken zipper can extend the life of many favorite garments. It is easy to replace a zipper because the original folds and stitching lines are already in position to guide every step.

The most common zipper ailments are teeth or coils that break in the middle of the zipper chain and sliders and pull tabs that separate from the zipper. These mishaps usually need a complete zipper replacement.

A zipper may break because it is not strong enough for its use or the fabric. Although coil zippers are lightweight and flexible, a metal or brass zipper may stand up better for heavy-duty wear.

Often the bottom of a separating zipper pulls loose from the garment. This can be repaired by replacing the stitching. Use thread that matches the color of the garment. As a reinforcement, stitch a bar tack at the bottom of the zipper (page 89).

Lengthening the zipper opening may be to your advantage. Most skirts and pants use 7" (18 cm) zippers, but an 8" or 9" (20.5 or 23 cm) zipper may provide just enough extra length to make the garment easier to get on and off. This will prevent putting too much strain on the bottom stop.

If metal zippers stick, rub beeswax or wax candle stub on the teeth to lubricate them. If metal teeth have rusted, place a drop of rust-eroding fluid on the rusted spot. Use paper towels under the zipper to absorb excess fluid.

To save wear and tear on the bottom stop, always close zippers before laundering and drycleaning.

Three Basic Steps to Replacing a Zipper

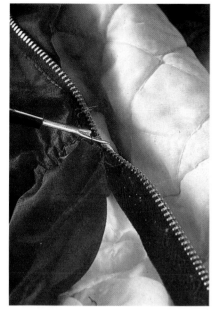

1) Remove zipper stitching with a seam ripper or point of sharp scissors, one or two stitches at a time. To avoid cutting fabric, do not slide seam ripper along seam. Also remove any stitching and fasteners that will interfere with zipper stitching.

2) Use a replacement zipper as similar as possible to original in color, weight and length. Preshrink zipper tape by soaking zipper in hot water for 30 minutes. Allow to air dry. Press tape with cool iron. Do not press over teeth.

3) Baste zipper in place with hand basting, pins, glue stick or basting tape. To machine-stitch close to zipper teeth, use zipper foot, which adjusts to either side of needle. Follow original stitching lines. Press lightly from right side, using a press cloth.

Two Ways to Shorten a Zipper

Shorten a zipper from top or bottom. Measure and mark correct length on longer zipper. Most zippers can be shortened from bottom. Fly-front and separating zippers are shortened from top to maintain bottom stop.

From the bottom. Line up tab of new zipper with tab of original. Zigzag or whipstitch several times over coil or teeth to form new bottom stop. Trim off excess zipper ½" (1.3 cm) below stitching.

From the top. Insert zipper before shortening, leaving excess zipper tape above opening. With zipper open, stitch across both ends of tape on original stitching line. Trim off excess zipper tape ½" (1.3 cm) above stitching line.

Lapped & Centered Zippers

Lightweight zippers are usually inserted with a lapped or centered application. The lapped zipper has a wide overlap on one side which covers the zipper teeth, and an underlap stitched close to the zipper teeth on the other side. A centered zipper is sewn in a seam with equal folds of fabric on each side of the zipper.

Either type of zipper may be inserted by hand or machine. The prickstitch is a couture technique used on fine designer clothing. Although the tiny stitches on the outside of the garment may look fragile, the long stitches on the underside are strong and secure enough to hold a zipper in place.

How to Insert a Zipper by Hand

1) **Follow** basic directions for replacing a lapped or centered zipper, opposite. After basting zipper in place, thread a fine needle with double all-purpose thread, silk thread or single strand of buttonhole twist; knot. Run thread over beeswax or white candle stub to strengthen and prevent tangling. Replace machine stitching with backstitch on underlap (page 57).

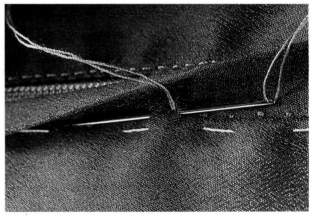

2) **Prickstitch** overlap. To prickstitch, bring needle through fabric to right side just below bottom stop. Insert needle two to three threads behind this point; bring it up ⅛" to ¼" (3 to 6 mm) in front of first stitch. Continue to top of zipper. Stitches on surface show as very small pricks.

How to Replace a Lapped Zipper

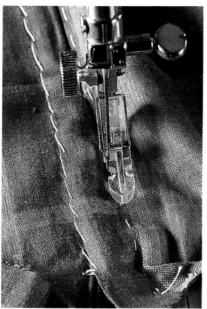

1) Baste zipper to underlap with teeth close to folded edge and bottom stop of zipper at seam opening. Attach zipper foot and adjust to left side of needle. Starting at bottom of zipper, stitch through underlap and zipper tape.

2) Baste overlap edge to stitching on underlap. Then baste other side of zipper in place just outside original stitching. Adjust zipper foot to right side of needle. Starting at bottom, stitch across and up on original stitching line.

3) Tuck zipper tape into the waistband or facing. Replace any stitching that was removed from waistband or facing using all-purpose presser foot.

How to Replace a Centered Zipper

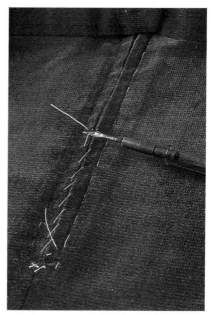

1) Open zipper. Position bottom stop at bottom of seam opening. Baste one side of zipper to one side of opening, positioning zipper teeth under folded edge so they are just covered. Close zipper.

2) Whipstitch edges together at center of zipper. Baste other side of zipper in place. Adjust zipper foot to right side of needle. Starting at top of zipper, stitch down one side, across bottom and up other side on original stitching lines.

3) Remove whipstitches. Tuck zipper tape into waistband or under facing. Align waistband or facing evenly on both sides. Restitch in place.

Separating & Fly-front Zippers

Several methods are used for inserting separating and fly-front zippers, so it is important to examine the original method of insertion closely before ripping out a zipper. Try to replace the zipper when you have uninterrupted sewing time available. It is easy to forget the order of the steps when there is a time lapse between work periods.

When replacing a separating zipper, remove the stitching from one side at a time. Then you will still have part of the original insertion in place to use as a guide for replacing linings and facings.

Note that in the fly-front zipper application the overlap side of the zipper is stitched to a facing, not to the garment. Topstitching holds the facing and zipper in place. On the right front of men's pants an extension may be a separate piece or cut in one piece with the garment and folded back. When a separate extension is used, the zipper is inserted between the extension and the outside of the pants, so only the zipper teeth are visible. When the extension is folded back, the zipper tape is stitched on top of it.

These instructions show the left front lapping over the right front as in men's pants. On women's pants the fly may lap the other direction.

How to Replace a Separating Zipper

 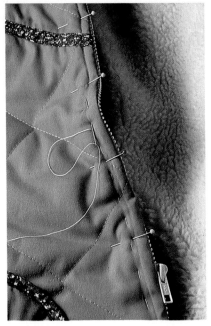 

1) Separate zipper. Place one side of zipper between jacket and facing with zipper tab toward outside of garment. Baste tape to facing only. Using zipper foot, stitch zipper to facing on basting line.

2) Pin jacket front over zipper. To hold securely for stitching, baste through all thicknesses. Using zipper foot, stitch on original zipper stitching line.

3) Zip both sides of zipper together to align jacket edges. Pin second side of zipper tape to facing; stitch, following steps 1 and 2, left. For added reinforcement, place a short bar tack across bottom of each zipper tape.

1) Mark overlap topstitching line with transparent tape or washable marking pen before removing zipper stitching. Remove topstitching. On inside, mark along edge of zipper tape for placement of new zipper. Remove zipper.

2) Open out facing on overlap. Baste zipper tape to facing along marked line on inside. Using zipper foot, stitch next to zipper teeth. Stitch again, ¼" (6 mm) from first row for reinforcement.

3) Open zipper. Pin folded edge of underlap over other side of zipper with fold along zipper teeth. Close zipper to check that it lies flat. Baste extension back in original position. Stitch through all thicknesses.

4) Shorten zipper from top, if necessary. Open zipper tab. Cut off top of zipper tapes ½" (1.3 cm) above original waistband stitching line. Tuck top ends into waistband. Replace waistband stitching.

5) Fold underlap extension back so it is out of the way. Using an all-purpose presser foot, replace topstitching on overlap side. Be careful not to catch extension in stitching line.

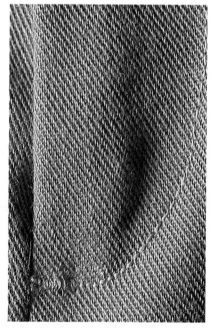

6) Replace bar tacks. Use narrow, closely spaced zigzag stitch ¼" to ½" (6 mm to 1.3 cm) long, directly below zipper stop. Be careful not to hit stop with needle. Bar tack may also be placed inside to hold facing and extension together.

Elastics

Frequent laundering with chlorine bleach and drying with high temperatures often cause elastics to wear out long before the garment. When the elastic loses its stretch, it needs replacing.

There are several types and widths of elastic, including the special-purpose elastic for lingerie and swimsuits. Woven or knitted elastic retains its width when stretched. Use it to replace elastic in a casing. Stronger than the woven or knitted elastic, braided elastic narrows when stretched. It, too, is used in casings. Lingerie elastic is soft and resilient. Sew it on the outside of the garment, away from the body, to prevent body oils and perspiration from damaging the elastic. Swimsuit elastic is braided and treated to resist chlorine.

To determine the amount of elastic needed, measure comfortably around part of body where it will be used. Add 1" (2.5 cm) for overlap. For waistbands, be sure the elastic will stretch over hips. When elastic is stitched to the garment instead of threaded through a casing, the stitching may stretch the elastic slightly. When measuring for stitched-on elastic, fit the elastic more snugly to allow for this extra stretch. For waistband elastics in lingerie, cut elastic 3" to 4" (7.5 to 10 cm) shorter than waist measurement.

Elastic in a casing that persists in twisting or curling can be remedied with a stitch-in-the-ditch technique, as shown below.

How to Prevent Twisted Elastic

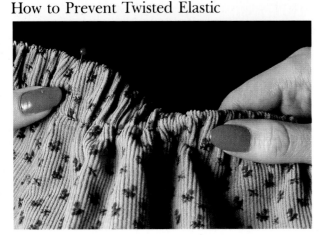

1) Straighten twisted or curled elastic by hand, feeling around entire casing and straightening as you go. Pin in straightened position at each seam, adjusting gathers evenly.

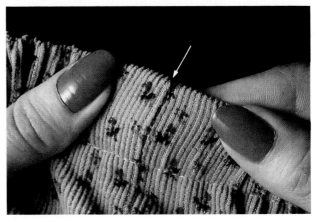

2) Stitch in the ditch (arrow) by machine or hand stitching exactly in the groove that is formed at the seam. Backstitch at each end of stitching or pull threads to wrong side and tie.

How to Replace Elastic in a Casing

1) Cut new elastic to appropriate length. At a seam, rip stitching from casing. If elastic has slipped into the center of the casing, use a loop turner or bodkin and grasp end of elastic with the hook.

2) Pin or tack one end of new elastic to original and pull through casing. Separate new elastic from original. Or pull new elastic through casing by attaching a safety pin or bodkin to the end and working it through the casing.

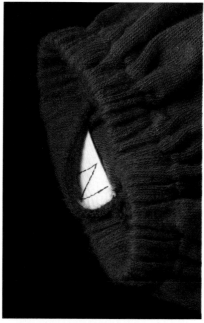

3) Overlap ends of newly encased elastic and stitch together by hand or machine. Ease elastic back into casing and restitch seam area where elastic was inserted. To prevent twisted elastic, follow steps 1 and 2, page 90.

How to Replace Elastic and Casing with Stretch Stitches

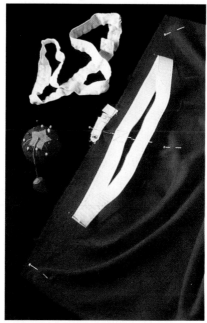

1) Remove stitching and elastic from casing. Use braided, non-roll elastic and determine appropriate length. Overlap ends 1" (2.5 cm) and stitch together. Divide elastic and casing area into four equal parts and mark each with pins.

2) Fold garment edge under the width of elastic plus ½" (1.3 cm). Press on fold line. Pin elastic inside casing, exactly on fold; match pins in elastic with garment. Stretch elastic (not the garment) and pin at 3" to 4" (7.5 to 10 cm) intervals.

3) Adjust machine to full-width blindstitch or stretch blind hemming stitch. From inside garment, stitch on hem next to elastic ridge; catch elastic only with widest stitch of the stitch pattern.

How to Replace Lingerie Elastic

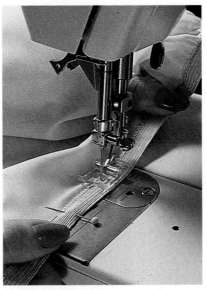

1) **Remove** original elastic. To shorten a half-slip, cut off at top to desired length plus ½" (1.3 cm) for seam. Cut ½" (1.3 cm) lingerie elastic 4" (10 cm) shorter than waist measurement. Butt ends together and zigzag. Divide elastic and waistline of slip into four equal parts and mark.

2) **Pin** straight edge of elastic on inside along cut edge, matching markings, with elastic joining at center back. Pin cut edge of 1½" (3.8 cm) length of ribbon between joining and slip. Stitch on picot edge of elastic, stretching elastic between pins.

3) **Turn** elastic to right side of garment. Zigzag or straight-stitch on straight edge of elastic. At joining, fold ribbon under the elastic. Using short straight stitches, stitch ribbon in a square over elastic joining.

How to Replace Encased Swimsuit Elastic

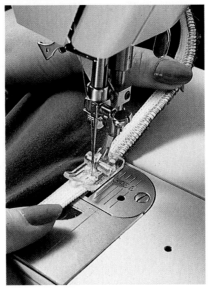

1) **Remove** stitching and original elastic. Cut appropriate length of chlorine-resistant elastic. Overlap ends and stitch together. Divide elastic and swimsuit edge into four equal parts and mark. Match elastic to swimsuit markings; pin to wrong side along cut edge.

2) **Stitch** elastic to swimsuit, stretching elastic between pins. Use a stretch stitch or narrow zigzag to sew edge of elastic to edge of swimsuit, stitching on outside edge of elastic.

3) **Fold** elastic under, toward garment, covering elastic. From the right side, use stretch stitch, zigzag or multi-stitch zigzag to stitch over previous stitching line. Stitch through casing and elastic.

Pockets

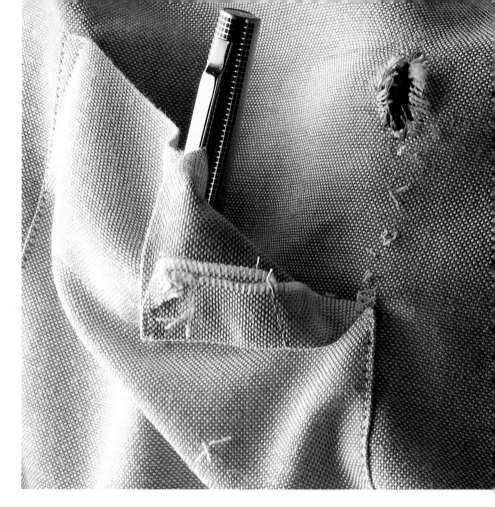

The most useful pockets on a garment are the ones most often in need of repair. Keys and other sharp objects can soon wear a hole in the side pockets of pants that are almost new. Bulging, overstuffed pockets can tear or weaken at the seams.

The technique for repair depends on whether the pocket is a patch pocket on the outside of the garment or a pocket lining hidden inside. Restitch a patch pocket in place. For pocket linings that are ripped or torn, restitch the lining or replace it with a purchased one.

Three Ways to Repair Pockets

Stitch pocket lining smaller to repair a small hole in the bottom. Machine-stitch just above the hole and trim off excess fabric. Finish raw edge with zigzag or overedge for fabrics that tend to ravel; trim edge with pinking shears for fabrics that do not ravel.

Repair worn pocket lining with a purchased iron-on pocket lining. Slide pocket replacement over outside of existing pocket. Fuse tape at top of pocket replacement to existing pocket. Hold iron in place for about 10 seconds. Trim existing pocket from inside ½" (1.3 cm) below fused tape.

Reinforce patch pocket that has ripped loose and torn the garment. Fuse a lightweight fabric or patch to wrong side of tear. Multi-stitch zigzag over tear if necessary. Restitch pocket in place on original seamline. Machine-stitch a triangle shape at each upper corner to reinforce pocket.

Vinyl, Leather, Suede & Nylon Fabrics

Vinyl, leather, suede and nylon require special techniques for repair. Because a hot iron cannot be used on these fabrics, fused repair is not possible. Instead, reinforce tears with fabric glue or adhesive. Special vinyl adhesives are also useful for some of the smooth-surfaced nylon fabrics.

Nylon taffeta and ripstop, used in skiwear, windbreakers, winter coats and snowsuits, are tightly woven to resist wind, water and abrasion. Nylon ripstop has a characteristic grid-like appearance and is usually lighter in weight than nylon taffeta, but nylon taffeta is stronger and less likely to sag. For garments that do not require drycleaning, fabric glue or nylon repair tape (available at sporting goods stores for sleeping bag and backpack repair) offer quick repair for these two fabrics.

How to Repair Tears and Holes in Vinyl

1) Cut a small patch of matching or lightweight woven fabric at least 1" (2.5 cm) larger than tear. Place it behind torn area.

2) Apply special liquid vinyl adhesive sparingly to torn edges; butt edges together.

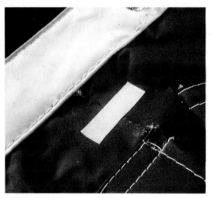

3) Place masking tape at right angles to tear to hold edges together while adhesive is drying. Remove excess adhesive with solvent.

How to Repair Tears and Holes in Nylon

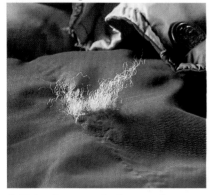

1) Trim loose ends from nylon fabric and backing.

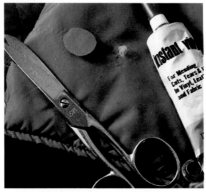

2) Cut and trim a patch of matching fabric to cover hole.

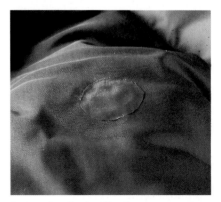

3) Apply vinyl adhesive to cut edges of patch and hole. Place patch over hole, allow adhesive to dry.

Furs & Pile Fabrics

Furs are most often used in coats, vests, jackets and trims. Fake furs and deep pile fabrics require repair techniques similar to furs.

Common areas in need of repair are closures and side-seam pockets. To attach buttons use a long thread shank (page 59) to accommodate the thickness of the fur or pile. Replace hook closures with covered hooks and eyes made especially for fur.

Splits in fur skins that occur with age are easy to repair. Small holes, too, are simple to hide if the hair of the fur is long. Use a heavy-duty size 7 glover's needle, or a wedge-shaped furrier's needle, and heavy-duty waxed thread for hand repairs.

How to Repair Tears in Furs

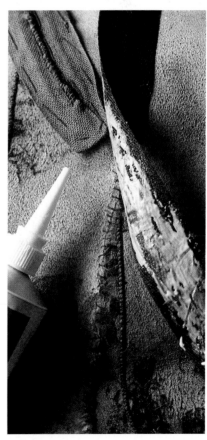

1) Butt edges of torn skin together, wrong side up. Push any exposed fur hairs to right side of skin with blunt end of needle.

2) Stitch two edges together, using waxed thread and furrier's needle. Make small stitches perpendicular to torn edges, inserting needle through both skins. Do not stitch through fur hairs.

3) Glue twill tape over seam to reinforce the repair. If fur is glazed, scrape off glaze before gluing tape.

Knits & Sweaters

Knit garments get frequent use, so they often need repair. Except for patching worn elbows or stitching split seams, which can be done by machine, most repairs to knit garments should be made by hand. Whatever method you use, allow for the stretch of the knit; otherwise, the repair will be obvious and it will not last long.

Repair ripped seams with a hand backstitch, whipstitch or machine stretch stitch. All three methods provide the stretchiness needed for knits.

If a yarn has pulled out of place but has not broken, repair the snag with a needle threader. If the yarn is broken, repair the hole with matching yarn or invisible nylon monofilament thread. Immediate repair prevents the hole from enlarging and developing a *run* (vertical rows of skipped stitching).

If waist, neck or sleeve ribbings of a sweater stretch out of shape, use elastic thread to regain resilient fit.

Three Ways to Repair Sweater Seams

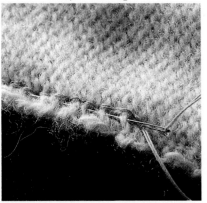

Backstitch by hand, using matching thread or yarn. To allow for give of knit, do not pull stitches too tight. To end, slip needle back through seam for about 2" (5 cm).

Whipstitch, using matching yarn. To begin, secure yarn with two small stitches and leave a 2" (5 cm) tail of yarn; whipstitch over it. To end, secure yarn and slip needle under whipstitches for 2" (5 cm).

Machine stretch-stitch to stitch and overcast edges at same time. Or, use forward/backward straight stretch stitch; then zigzag edges together with narrow zigzag.

How to Fix Snags

1) Insert wire point of needle threader from wrong side so point emerges on right side exactly at snag. Thread snagged yarn through eye of needle threader.

2) Pull wire end of needle threader back to inside of sweater or knit garment. Do not cut off excess yarn of snag.

3) Stretch sweater gently on each side of snag to reposition pulled yarns. It may be necessary to pull up loops on wrong side with eye of a needle.

How to Repair Runs

1) Pick up loop at bottom of run with a crochet hook, working from right side of garment. With first loop on hook, bring hook through loose stitch above.

2) Pull loose stitch through loop. Repeat until you reach broken yarns at top of run.

3) Pull the two broken ends of yarn through the top loop.

4) Pull each broken yarn to the inside through the next stitch above on each side.

5) Thread needle with matching thread. Whipstitch two yarn ends together with tiny stitches. If necessary, close hole with small stitches from wrong side.

How to Reshape Stretched Ribbing with Elastic Thread

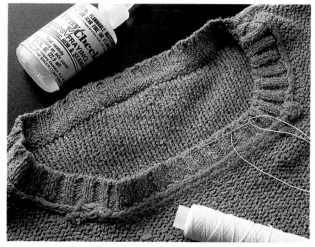 

1) Secure elastic thread on wrong side at seam. Use liquid fray preventer on cut ends of thread to prevent raveling, or knot thread. Take small running stitches from one rib to next, being careful that stitches do not show on outside of garment.

2) Stitch additional rows of elastic thread about ½" (1.3 cm) apart if needed on waist and cuff. Secure each row. Do not pull elastic too tight; ease ribs together evenly.

Customizing

Customizing for Fit & Fashion

Even with an organized closet and a conscientious routine of care and repair, you may still have clothes that you rarely wear. In the back of your closet may be an unflattering blouse, a skirt that does not fit comfortably, or a coat with fashion details from a decade past. By customizing, you can update the style of your clothes and adjust their fit. Sometimes the simplest change makes a big difference.

Customizing offers many personal rewards. With a little imagination you can alter an ill-fitting dress, recycle an out-of-date sweater, restyle a suit bought at a garage sale or change any garment in your closet to better suit your taste.

Customizing is also a good way to economize. Adjustments in length or style can eliminate the need for a new jacket or coat, for example.

Before making any changes, first identify why you do not wear the garment. Whether the problem is fit or style, consider it carefully to determine possible changes that offer a solution.

Whether you're altering or updating, also consider the amount of time needed for the project. Shortening a skirt usually takes less time than narrowing the lapels of a jacket. Simple changes can often be made quickly, whereas larger projects may require planning.

Finally, consider your options. Once you decide to recycle your clothing, you will find many alternatives:

- Alter a garment that does not fit. It may be necessary to change the width by taking a seam in or letting one out, or the length by moving a hemline up or down.

- Change the style of a garment to get the fit you want if an alteration in length or width is not possible. If the sleeves of a sweater are too short, the solution may be to turn the sweater into a vest.

- Update or individualize a garment by making simple changes in the styling. The changes may be as easy as adding trimming or changing the buttons. Be imaginative in finding ways to give new life to your clothes.

- Change the use of the garment if no other option is available. When the fabric is still in good condition, make something else from it after detaching buttons, zippers and usable trimmings. Fabric from an adult's garment may be ideal for making a jumper or pants for a child.

Analyze the Fit

If the problem with a garment is poor fit, take time to further pinpoint what's wrong with the fit. Try on the garment, wearing the shoes, undergarments and other accessories that you plan to use with it. Take a good look in a full-length mirror.

Examine problems with the fit, such as wrinkles, sagging, bagging, pulling and gapping, and identify their causes. Also check the seams of the garment and grainlines of the fabric. The seams of a well-fitting garment fall naturally along body lines. The lengthwise grain of the fabric should be vertical; the crosswise grain should be horizontal without any areas being pulled out of alignment. Finally, and most important, consider the comfort. The garment should feel good as well as look good.

Use the following standards for comparing the garment's actual fit to the ideal fit.

Neckline fits without pulling or gapping. Collar lies smooth and flat, or stands, hugging the back of the neck, as designed.

Shoulder and armhole seamlines wrap the curves of the body comfortably. Shoulder seam lies directly on top of the shoulder. Natural armhole seam begins at the end of the shoulder and is straight above the underarm curve. For broad or padded shoulder style, armhole seam extends 1" to 2" (2.5 to 5 cm).

Bustline darts, if any, point to the fullest part of the bust. Garment with front opening has a button or other closure at bust level. Closing does not pull or gap at bustline.

Waistline seam or band falls at the body's natural waistline, depending on the garment. It wraps the waist comfortably, allowing room for breathing and movement.

Hip area rests smoothly on the body without pulling and wrinkling. Side seams hang perpendicular to the floor. Check closures and pocket openings for wrinkles, pulling and other signs of stress.

Skirt length is flattering to you and appropriate to the fashion look you wish to achieve. Unless the hemline is shaped, it is even and parallel to the floor.

Pants length is appropriate for style of pants. Man-tailored pants should extend to the top of the heel in back and touch the top of the shoe in front.

Making the Change

When customizing clothes, you will probably use many of the tools already in your repair kit, especially the seam ripper, measuring tools, pins and chalk. Collect odds and ends of notions, such as buttons, trimmings and seam tapes, and keep them handy for updating garments.

Your alteration or update will be most successful if the garment that you are changing meets certain requirements. Be sure you have adequate seam allowances or hems to work with, the fabric is in satisfactory condition, the garment design lends itself to change and the alteration/makeover project is not too ambitious for your sewing skills.

Seam allowances. If you need to add extra width to a garment, it should have adequate seam allowances. In many purchased garments, seam allowances are narrow with finished edges that may fray when stitching is removed. If a seam allowance is narrower than 1/4" (6 mm), it can be extended with seam binding or twill tape.

Fabric condition. Check fabric for damage from stitching that you remove. Look for any permanent creases or signs of wear around fabric edges. Also, the exposed surface of some fabrics may have faded; covered areas, such as in a seam or a pleat, may be a darker shade if uncovered. It may be necessary to work around fabric flaws by changing the design or camouflaging with topstitching or trimmings.

Garment design. Proportions and design lines should remain pleasing after the alteration. Look at the complexity of details and seam lines. Some alterations may require crossing several seams and disturbing the details. Simpler designs offer less chance of problems.

When deciding whether or not to make an alteration, keep these points in mind.

- It is usually easier to take in seams than to let them out.

- Drastic changes in size may be impractical.

- Alterations in the neckline, bustline, shoulder, underarm and crotch are more difficult than alterations in uncurved areas.

- After making one alteration, try on the garment before making other changes. The first alteration may correct more than one problem.

- Remember, if an alteration to correct garment fit is not possible, it may still be possible to restyle the garment. For example, a dress that is too short may be cut off and made into a skirt or shirt.

General Reminders

The sewing techniques for alterations are much the same as in other sewing projects. Pay special attention to these reminders:

- Wash or clean the garment before making the alteration. If the garment is new, it may shrink slightly, which may change the amount of alteration needed. If the garment has been worn, cleaning will remove soil so it does not get pressed or sewn into the clothing. For a hem change, release the hem before cleaning.

- Look closely at the garment construction. Try to duplicate thread color, topstitching and construction methods.

- When making the alteration, press often, just as you would with any other sewing project. It is especially important to press well before crossing a seam with a new sewing line.

How to Remove Stitching

Chain stitching. Clip a stitch and pull the thread to the right. These stitches are often used for hems in manufactured garments.

Straight stitching. On one side of seam, cut threads with seam ripper every ½" to 1" (1.3 to 2.5 cm). Keep fabric stable, being careful not to stretch fabric or cut fabric yarns. From other side, pull thread.

How to Remove Crease and Stitching Lines

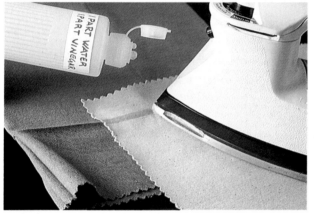

Stubborn creases. Dampen the crease with a solution of equal parts of white vinegar and water. Press with a damp cloth.

Stitching lines. To close the holes left in fabric from the original seam, press using a damp cloth.

How to Mark and Fit with Pins

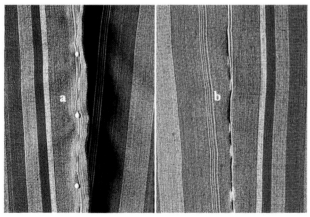

Mark. On right sides **(a)** mark new seamline with pins in exact location of new seam. Turn garment to inside. Using pins as a guide, **(b)** mark new stitching lines with chalk or marking pen.

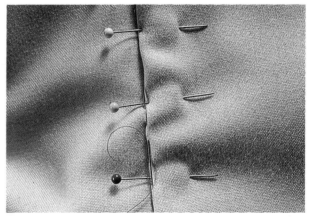

Fit. Insert pins perpendicular to seamline to hold fabric smooth and let you see how the new seam will look when stitched. From right side, slip-baste layers together. Remove pins. Turn garment to inside and stitch through center of basting.

Changing the Length

Fashion trends in hemlines seem to change almost every season. Purchased clothing often needs an adjustment to personalize the length. For these reasons, the most common of all clothing alterations is a change in the hem. It is also one of the easiest alterations. Whether the garment length is to move up or down, the general process remains the same.

Release the original hem in the garment and press with a damp cloth to remove the crease. If you are lengthening the garment and the crease is visible after pressing, stitch trimming over the line, or topstitch with double needle or decorative stitch. Repeat this detail on another area of the garment.

Try on the garment, wearing the shoes you intend to wear with it. Mark the new garment length, using a skirt marker or yardstick to ensure an even hem. Turn up the garment at the new hemline. Baste or press the folded edge. Grade seam allowances inside the hem, if needed, to reduce bulk.

Adjust the hem depth, as determined by fabric, style and fullness of the garment. Hem depths are often 3" (7.5 cm) for children's dresses, gathered or straight skirts; 2" (5 cm) for slightly flared skirts; and 1" (2.5 cm) or less for flared and circular skirts. An average pants hem depth is 1½" (3.8 cm).

Easestitch the hem edge to adjust for excess fullness, or release at the side seams if more fullness is needed on the tapered edges. Finish the hem edge with the same finish as the original hem or with seam tape (page 81).

Pin the hem in place and stitch with a hand or machine hemming stitch (page 81). For a hand-stitched hem, use an even, loose stitch, being careful the stitches do not show on the outside of the garment.

If you need to lengthen a garment but the hem allowance is not deep enough, insert a band of matching or contrasting fabric above the hemline. Make the finished band the width needed for garment length, plus seam allowances.

Coordinate with another band on a different part of the garment. A skirt may be given extra length by adding a band of fabric or a ruffle to the lower edge of the hem. Repeat the detail on a sleeve, neckline or collar.

A skirt may also be shortened at the waistline. This method may be necessary when a skirt is extremely full, or when the hem is permanently pleated or has a border design so the length cannot be changed at the lower edge.

How to Lengthen with a Facing

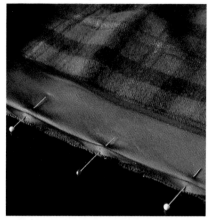

1) Use purchased 2" (5 cm) wide bias binding to lengthen a hem its maximum amount. With right sides together, pin bias binding to cut edge, raw edges even.

2) Stitch on foldline of binding. Grade seam by trimming binding close to stitching line.

3) Press binding to inside on a line about ⅛" to ¼" (3 to 6 mm) from seam. Ease bias binding to fit garment. Hem with slipstitch (page 81).

How to Shorten

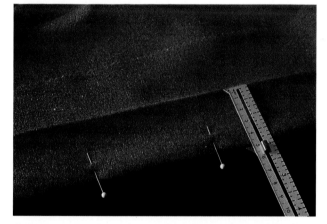

1) Measure and mark new hemline, using original hemline as guide. If original hemline is uneven, measure with skirt marker. Pin new hem in place.

2) Trim off excess hem allowance. Trim seam allowances in hem area to reduce bulk. Complete basic hemming procedure (page 81).

Common Errors in Hemming

Hem too deep. Hem was stitched before being trimmed to correct hem depth. This adds excess bulk and weight, and is unattractive on right side.

Hem turned twice. Original hem was turned under two or more times. This creates a bulky ridge that is obvious on the right side of the garment.

How to Shorten a Skirt at the Waistline

1) **Try on** skirt and mark desired garment length. Measure between lower edge and desired length to determine amount to be shortened.

2) **Mark** the amount to be shortened down from the waist seam at the top of the skirt.

3) **Remove** waistband and zipper, noting original construction. Cut away excess fabric, ½" (1.3 cm) above marked line to allow for waistband seam.

4) **Gather or pleat** upper edge of skirt to fit waistband, duplicating original construction. To replace zipper, extend opening. Reattach waistband.

How to Shorten a Cuffed Sleeve

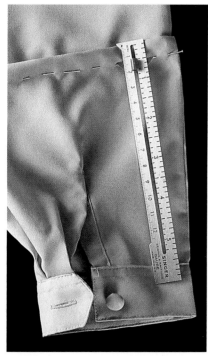

1) Mark correct sleeve length by pinning a tuck around the sleeve. Measure the tuck, which is half the amount to be shortened.

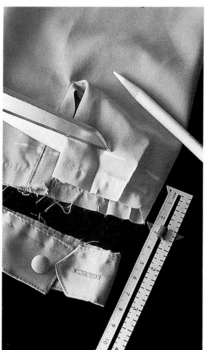

2) Remove the cuff, noting original construction and seam allowance. Remove placket if length change requires. Trim sleeve the amount to be shortened.

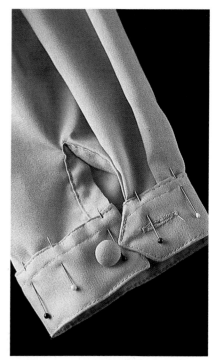

3) Gather or pleat edge of sleeve to fit cuff. If placket was removed, reattach. Reattach cuff.

How to Shorten a Tapered Pants or Sleeve Edge

1) Fold up hem to desired length. Trim hem depth. Check to see that hem lies flat. Puckers indicate hem is narrower than hemming line.

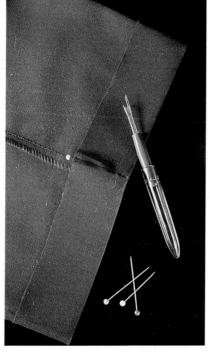

2) Release stitching if necessary to eliminate puckers. Starting at hem foldline, taper new seamlines out to widen pants or sleeve hem edge.

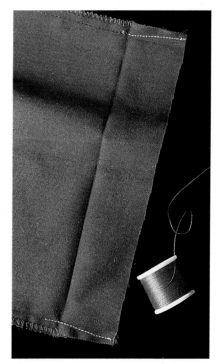

3) Stitch new seams so width of hem edge is same as hemming line. When more than one seam is involved, distribute change equally. Replace hem.

Taking In & Letting Out

To personalize the fit, it is often necessary to alter the width by taking in or letting out the seams. This is a simple alteration to make in seams that do not have pockets or zippers. Distribute adjustments in width evenly around the garment, dividing the amount of change needed by the number of seams involved. Measure and stitch accurately because a small amount can make a big difference in the fit. For example, a ¼" (6 mm) change in two seams will change the measurement by 1" (2.5 cm).

How to Take In a Seam

1) Try on garment. With aid of a friend, pin out excess fabric, distributing adjustments evenly among seams. To reach the seam needing adjustment, you may need to rip a seam that crosses it. If not, wait to remove original stitching until new stitching is complete. Mark new seamline on inside of garment.

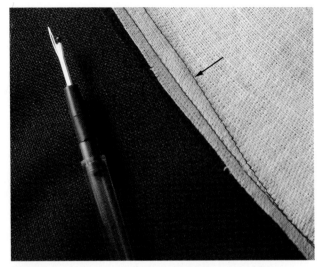

2) Pin and stitch new seam (arrow) at markings, matching thread and stitch length to original. Blend stitching into original seamline, overlapping 1" (2.5 cm) at each end. Trim excess fabric, keeping seam allowances a consistent width. Apply seam finish compatible with fabric and original finish.

How to Let Out a Seam

1) Check seam allowances to be sure that they are wide enough to let out. Release seams amount needed for adjustment. Try on garment and repin seams as in step 1, above. To extend seam allowance, stitch twill tape or seam binding on seam edge. Steam press seam allowances flat.

2) Pin and stitch new seams as marked. Blend stitching into original seamline, overlapping stitching for 1" (2.5 cm) at each end of seam. If seams have not been extended with tape or binding, use liquid fray preventer on narrow seams to prevent raveling.

How to Adjust a Man-tailored Waistband

1) Try on pants and mark amount of change needed by pinning out excess at center back. Mark seam on inside (page 103).

2) Remove the belt loop and the waistband facing at center back. Release center back seam the amount needed. Press flat.

3) Pin and stitch the center back seam and facings along the new seam line.

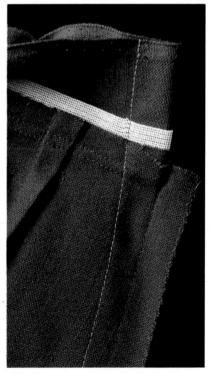

4) Trim excess fabric, if necessary, leaving enough to let out again. Finish seam allowances if trimmed.

5) Press the facing back in place and stitch, matching the original construction. Replace belt loop.

Pants without center waistband seam may also be taken in by this method. Extend center back seam through waistband. Trim and finish edges.

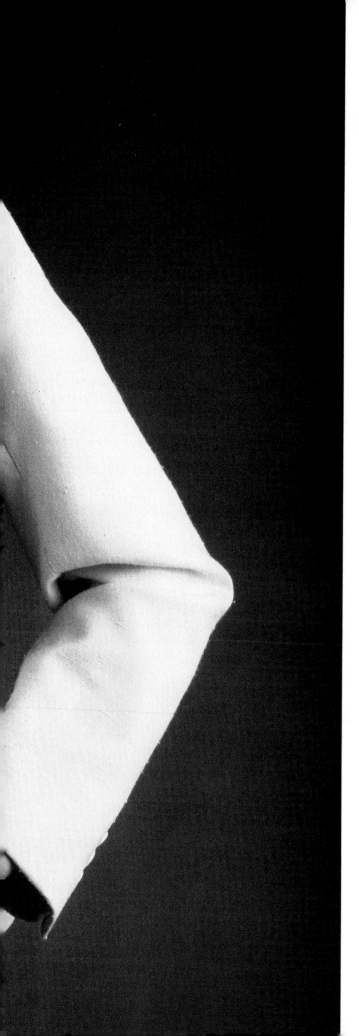

Updating

Updating your wardrobe is one way to stay current with clothing styles without buying or sewing new garments with every fashion change. A major element of clothing is the silhouette, or outline of the garment. Change the silhouette of a dress and you may change its style.

You may need to change only one area of a garment to update its style. Pants and dresses may require only an alteration in the hemline. Necklines are focal points that may become dated as styles change. Sometimes all a jacket or shirt needs is an update in the collar or lapels.

Updating can be creative and rewarding. Consider making changes that result in simple, classic styling to extend the fashion wearability; or make a trendy update for fun.

Keep in mind the total garment when you are making changes in the design. What you do to one part will affect the visual appeal of the whole. Whenever you add fabric or trim to a garment, you may also be adding new texture or color. Repeat design details to coordinate the texture, color or other style features of the garment. If you are adding rows of topstitching around a skirt hemline, consider topstitching at the neck edge or sleeve hems, too.

Check the garment for limitations and possibilities. Think of several possible solutions to a style problem before choosing one. Consider making changes in one or more of the following ways.

Use. Restyle pants into shorts, or a dress into a blouse or skirt. Redesign a sweater into a vest. Restyle an adult's garment into one for a child, or make a new garment from the fabric.

Silhouette. Reshape a garment. Create a waistline. Narrow pants legs that are too wide. Narrow shoulders of a dress or blouse by adding tucks or gathers.

Neck and sleeve edges. Remove or reshape a collar. Replace a collar or cuffs with knitted ribbing. Update a suit by narrowing the lapels. Restyle long sleeves into short sleeves.

Details. Add an applique, ribbon, buttons, pockets or other trim. Replace original buttons or trim. Or remove trim that detracts from the design of the garment or dates it.

Shortening a Dress to a Shirt

Making a shirt or blouse from a dress can be as easy as sewing a new hem. If the dress is too short or the hip area is too tight, simply shorten the dress to tunic or blouse length. If the dress fits well but still receives little wear, shortening it may increase its usefulness in your wardrobe.

A dress without a waistline is ideal for this project. The fabric and design features of the dress determine whether the resulting garment is a tailored shirt or dressy blouse. A knit dress can be shortened to a versatile T-shirt.

Try on the dress and mark the new shirt length. You may wish to use a shirt or blouse of a similar style as a guideline when choosing the length. Cut away the excess fabric, allowing for a hem. Finish the hem with machine topstitching.

Restyling a Dress to a Skirt

To restyle a dress to a skirt, remove the bodice and finish the waistline area. A dress without a waistline is a good candidate for this makeover.

You may choose to restyle the dress if it fits poorly through the bodice or sleeves, has outdated design details in the neck or sleeve area, or shows signs of wear or damage in the bodice area. It may be necessary to remove pockets or add a zipper or buttons for a new waistband closure.

Try on the dress. Tie a string around your waist, adjusting skirt to the desired length so original hem can be maintained. Mark the new waistline at the string. Cut above the mark, allowing for a casing or seam at the waistline. Finish the top edge with a casing and elastic (page 91). Or cut a waistband from excess fabric.

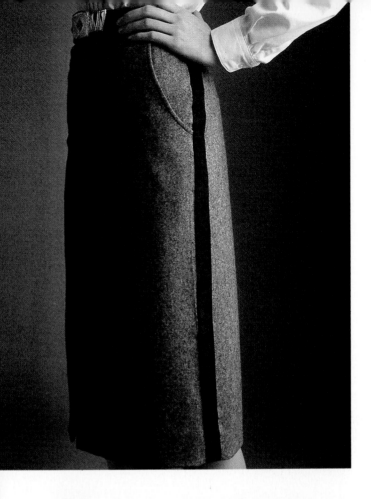

Redesigning Skirts

Skirts offer many possibilities for updating because their basic shapes are uncomplicated. Restyling can also correct problems in fit such as side-seam pockets that pull because the skirt is too tight across the hips. To loosen the fit, add a tuxedo stripe down the sides.

Lengthen a skirt by adding bands of contrasting fabric, either flat or ruffled. Extend a skirt from the top with the addition of a yoke.

Add fullness or flare to a skirt by opening seams and inserting panels. Or take out fullness to create a slimmer silhouette. Change a pleated skirt to a gathered one by removing the waistband and readjusting. Or replace gathers with pleats.

How to Add a Tuxedo Stripe to a Skirt

1) Try on the skirt. Correct for tightness in hip area by opening the side seams and releasing the waistband stitching above seams. Overlap seam allowances to expanded position; taper to original width at waist. Pin and baste.

2) Place a band of ribbon, synthetic suede or other trim down the sides of the skirt over exposed seam, tucking upper edge of band under waistband. Topstitch edges. Replace waistband stitching.

How to Restyle an A-line Skirt to a Straight Skirt

1) Remove the hem. Try on the skirt inside out. Pin out the excess fullness at seams, removing equal amounts from each side.

2) Stitch along new seamlines. Finish seam allowances and add topstitching for new design detail. Hem (page 81).

How to Restyle a Wrap Skirt to a Button-front Skirt

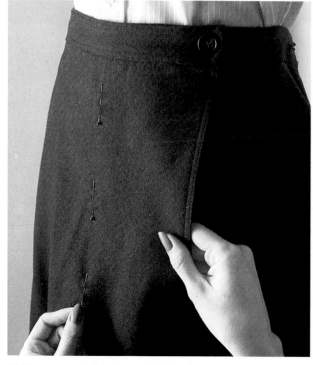

1) Remove stitching at waistband front to release any gathers. Try on the skirt, and pin closed at a comfortable position. On both layers of fabric, mark a line down the center front.

2) Cut away excess garment, allowing 1" (2.5 cm) for overlap and 2" (5 cm) for turned-back facing on each side. Turn facing under on each center front edge. Match center front markings. Finish waistband. Add buttonholes on overlap, buttons on underlap.

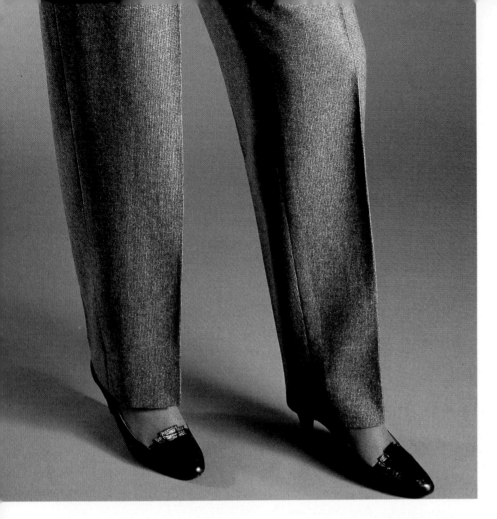

Narrowing Pants Legs

Just as hemlines go up and down, the width of pants legs varies with fashion, ranging from full to narrow. A wide leg may be changed to a narrower width simply by sewing new seamlines. An adjustment in width may also require a change in length.

Pants seams with little or no detail are the easiest to change. Flat-felled seams, such as those on jeans, and topstitched seams require extra care to duplicate.

For the pants leg to fit correctly, the lengthwise grain should hang at right angles to the floor with equal amounts removed from the inseam and the outseam. If all the narrowing is done in one seam, the grainline will twist around the leg.

How to Narrow Pants Legs

1) Remove hem. Measure and mark new width at hemline, removing equal amounts from inseam and outseam.

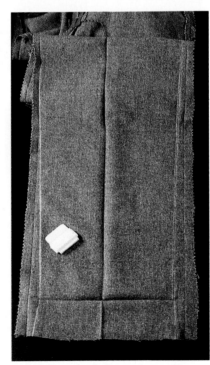

2) Mark and stitch new seamlines. Start at knee area or above and taper to mark at hem. Adjust hem to fit pants leg (page 82).

3) Remove original stitching. Trim and finish seams if necessary. Hem with machine blindstitch.

Shortening Pants to Shorts

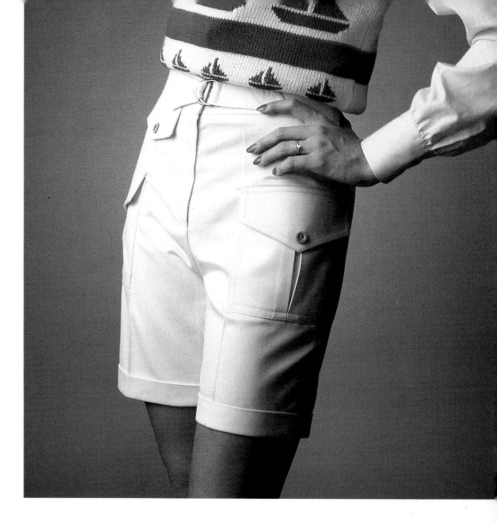

You can update the pants in your wardrobe by changing their length. Shortening pants is an easy restyling project.

Pants that fit loosely in the leg may be shortened to culottes. Or gather the fabric into a band below the knee for knickers. Another variation is to add a cuff, at any length, from matching or contrasting fabric; use leftover fabric to add details such as pockets. Besides changing the length, you may need to reshape the leg or hemline.

How to Restyle Pants into Cuffed Shorts

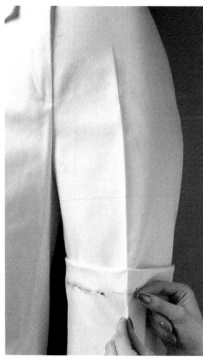

1) Try on pants. Determine and mark new length, folding up a cuff if desired.

2) Cut off excess fabric, allowing for hem. Press hem and cuff in position. Finish edge. Hem with machine straight stitch.

3) Use leftover fabric from pants leg to make pockets, tabs or other design details.

Changing Collars & Necklines

Often the neckline of a garment provides the main design interest. By changing it, you can transform the whole look. For a quick update, reshape the collar. For a major change, completely restyle it. For example, long ties at the neckline can be removed and changed to a lapped collar band with a front placket.

If the collar detracts from the design of the garment or fits too tightly, remove it and design a new neckline, or replace the collar. Consider adding a lace collar, a collar of a contrasting color, a stand-up ribbed band or a purchased knit collar.

Determine what effect the change will have on the total garment. To be compatible with the new design, other details such as buttons or trim may need to be changed.

How to Remove Ties from a Collar

1) Cut away tie on left side ½" (1.3 cm) beyond facing edge. Turn cut edge to inside. Slipstitch. Cut off right tie ¼" (6 mm) from facing edge.

2) Form band down center front by laying tie over right front matching edges. Baste; edgestitch on inside edge of band.

3) Form small pleats in right edge of collar. Baste. Tuck pleated edge into top of new front band. Slipstitch in place.

How to Reshape a Collar

1) Mark new design line with pins along upper layer of collar. Remove collar from neckband. Remove topstitching.

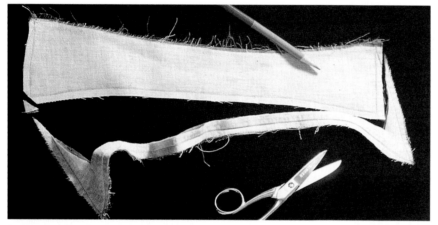

2) Turn collar inside out. Mark inside of collar with marking pencil, using pins as a guideline. Stitch along new design line. Trim excess fabric.

3) Sew collar back onto the neckband, and topstitch. Use the same procedure for narrowing collars of other styles.

How to Remove a Collar and Change a Neckline

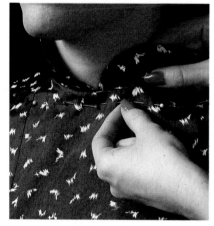

1) Try on garment and mark new neckline with pins. Cut away collar and excess fabric, allowing ½" (1.3 cm) for seam.

2) Cut a facing from a compatible fabric or use bias tape to finish edge. Stitch facing or tape to neck edge, trim to ¼" (6 mm), press and understitch.

3) Add a button and buttonhole, or other closure, at top of neckline if needed.

Narrowing Lapels

Because the shape and width of collars and lapels vary with fashion, these details can quickly date a garment. Narrowing the lapels of a suit jacket or blazer is a common updating project.

This project can be challenging for the novice sewer. Suit jackets and blazers include a variety of construction techniques, such as topstitching, felted undercollars and hand padstitching. Whatever the combination of techniques in your jacket, the general procedures for alteration are similar.

Lapels can be narrowed by hand or by machine. These instructions show the hand method on the collar and the machine method on the lapels. Choose the method or combination that will work best for your project.

Look carefully at the original shape of the collar and lapels. To retain a pleasing proportion, both areas may need adjustment. The collar may need to be shortened, as well as narrowed, to retain a deep notch where it is joined to the lapel.

How to Narrow Lapels

1) Mark new shape of lapel and collar on upper layer with basting stitches. Use contrasting thread. Fabrics may also be marked with chalk or marking pen.

2) Shorten collar by removing stitches from lapel/collar seam to ½" (1.3 cm) beyond new design line. Cut away excess fabric, allowing ¼" (6 mm) for seam. Remove topstitching.

3) Turn under and press the upper layer of collar along new seamline. Cut away excess interfacing to seamline. Press under seam allowance of undercollar.

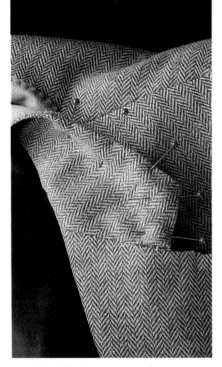

4) Pin collar layers together, adjusting, if necessary, so the undercollar does not show from the outside.

5) Stitch edges together by hand, using small slipstitches in matching thread. If collar was shortened, slipstitch lapel/collar seam together.

6) Release hem of jacket lining enough to allow you to reach lapels.

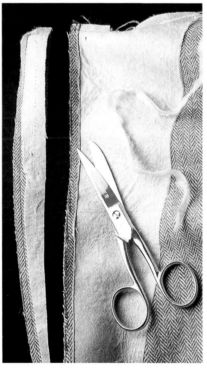

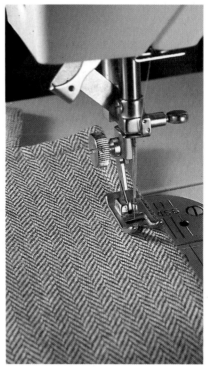

7) Turn garment inside out at lapel area. Following basted seamline, mark new stitching line.

8) Machine-stitch lapels and lapel facings together along new seamline. Trim away interfacing. Press seams open.

9) Turn jacket right side out. Carefully press collar and lapels, checking that underedges do not show. Topstitch if necessary to match original design.

Restyling Sweaters

Sweaters can easily be restyled for a fresh update or creative repair. You may simply change the neckline or you may choose a more challenging makeover such as creating a vest. Whatever the project, sweaters generally show big rewards for little effort.

Restyling offers many variations. Try mixing fabrics, trims and yarns. Add a yoke of synthetic suede, for instance. Choose from several methods to finish the edges of a restyled sweater. Use excess fabric to trim new edges; for example, trim a makeover V-neck with leftover ribbing from a turtleneck. Replace cuffs and waistband with purchased ribbing, or consider adding a casing and elastic. Edges may also be trimmed with crochet or knit stitches in a matching or contrasting yarn.

Save discarded sweater pieces for other projects. Use the sleeves for a quick makeover into leg warmers; finish the cut edge with a casing and elastic. Mittens can be made from sweater scraps, too.

How to Change a Sweater to a Vest

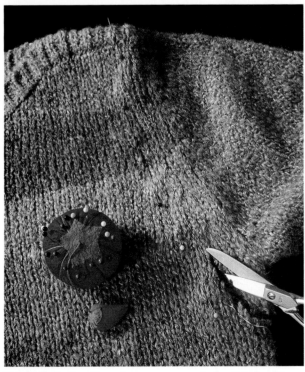

1) Mark design line along new armhole. Stitch ½" (1.3 cm) out from this line. Cut ¼" (6 mm) from stitching line.

2) Finish new edges by encasing with bias tricot binding. Turn edges under along new design lines and slipstitch in place.

How to Change a Pullover to a Cardigan

1) Stitch two rows of straight stitches down the center front, following the lengthwise rib. This stabilizes the knit loops and keeps them from pulling out. Cut between the stitching lines.

2) Finish the new edges by applying preshrunk grosgrain ribbon, being careful not to stretch the sweater. The ribbon may be applied on the inside or outside. Add buttonholes, and buttons.

How to Change a Turtleneck to a Crew Neck

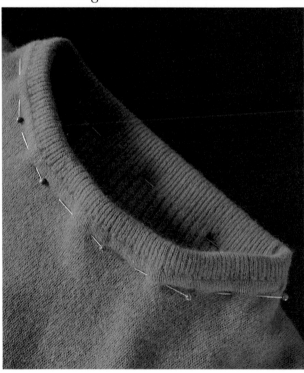

1) Fold excess turtleneck fabric to inside, forming a crew neck of desired width. Pin or baste.

2) Stitch in the ditch where collar joins neckline. Add a second row of stitching if desired; trim away excess fabric.

Index

COWBOY ETHICS

What Wall Street Can Learn from the Code of the West

AUTHOR **JAMES P. OWEN**

PHOTOGRAPHER **DAVID R. STOECKLEIN**

COLLABORATING WRITER **BRIGITTE LEBLANC**

ART DIRECTOR | DESIGNER **NITA ALVAREZ**

EDITOR **CARRIE LIGHTNER**

STOECKLEIN PUBLISHING & PHOTOGRAPHY

Tenth Street Center   Suite A1

Post Office Box 856   Ketchum, Idaho 83340

tel 208.726.5191   *fax* 208.726.9752

toll-free 800.727.5191   *web* www.drsphoto.net

This book is dedicated to
the memory of my father,

DR. JAMES F. OWEN

In the years since he passed away,
I've often wondered what I would say to my father
if I somehow had the chance to see him once more.
Because of this project, I now know that I would say,
"Dad, you were always my hero."

AUTHOR'S NOTE

WHY THIS BOOK

After thirty-five years in the investment management industry, I can tell you that it runs on brains, nerve, and ambition. This business doesn't often give you the chance to do something from the heart. But I am taking that chance now, because the subject of our industry's ethics and values has become my consuming passion.

Not so many years ago, the denizens of Wall Street inspired awe and envy. We were "masters of the universe" and had the numbers to prove it. But after a wave of scandals exposed a dark side of the industry, I found myself mourning what had been lost. I could only wonder: How did we get to this sorry state? When did we stop caring about our principles and the well-being of our clients? And most importantly, how could we begin to redeem ourselves and earn back the trust of investors and regulators? Our malady was so deep-rooted that I could see no cure.

A little more than a year ago, almost by accident, my troubled musings on the state of our industry came together with my lifelong interest in the Old West and the era of the open range. Suddenly I found my source of inspiration: the real-life working cowboy. I spent the next year exploring the life and code of the working cowboy and distilling the principles of what I call Cowboy Ethics.

Spreading this word has now become my calling. In fact, I see it as the culmination of my career; I feel as though everything I have ever done has led me to this point. While I am still an active partner in my firm, a hedge fund of funds advisor based in Austin, Texas, my career emphasis has shifted.

Now, when I think about how I would like to be remembered, it is not as the guy who lived in a beautiful house or brought in a lot of business or helped to build investment firms ~ though I have done all those things. I would rather be known as the guy who was not embarrassed or afraid to speak up about issues that matter a great deal. I have come to realize that anybody can make money; it is much harder to make a difference. That is what I hope Cowboy Ethics will do.

By no means is Cowboy Ethics the last word on Wall Street ethics; I am not that naïve. But I am optimistic. I believe Cowboy Ethics can be a profound source of inspiration for meaningful change that starts with individuals, percolates through firms and organizations, and could ultimately help transform the industry at large. Wall Street desperately needs a way out of its morass. Cowboy Ethics is a place we can start.

JAMES P. OWEN

Santa Barbara, California

FOREWORD

People often ask me what it is about cowboys that makes them so different from the rest of us. They want to know why the West and cowboys stand out as symbols of American culture and values. In my mind, it is because cowboys live by the Code of the West, a code of honor and truthfulness. They live in a world where a man's word is his bond and a handshake is enough to seal any agreement.

The West is a place where the fence is always tight but the gate is always open to friends and neighbors. It is a place where a man can make tough decisions without looking over his shoulder or worrying what someone else will think. A cowboy gets his strength from knowing what is right and what is wrong and being true to his beliefs. This is the essence of the Code of the West and the true cowboy way.

I am proud to be a part of the culture of the West and feel lucky to be able to live in such a beautiful environment. I love riding horses and pushing cattle under the Western skies. I work side by side with men who live and breathe the Code of the West and who share an undying love of the land. For them, cowboying is not just a job, but a way of life.

For the past 20 years, I have dedicated my life to photographing cowboys and cowgirls as they work and play throughout the West. It has been my goal to preserve the West on film and present these images to the world through the pages of my books and calendars.

I am honored to have my work published in this volume, Cowboy Ethics, *because the Western images tie in so perfectly with the text. You might not think that the West and Wall Street go together, but in many ways they do. Like cowboys, the men and women of Wall Street are risk-takers, yet they are also accountable for the results they deliver. Like investment professionals who must constantly make high-stakes decisions, a cowboy lays it all on the line every day. He knows that at any time, his horse can step in a hole and fall and kill him, or his cattle can get caught in a snowstorm and freeze to death. A true cowboy is someone others can count upon in any situation, no matter how rocky. In the same way, investors must know they can trust their advisors to do right by them through both good times and bad.*

People on Wall Street and cowboys share a can-do spirit and an ever-present sense of optimism. They also share a tradition of hard work, resourcefulness, and perseverance. Jim Owen has done a wonderful job of tying these themes together. His vision for preserving a code of ethics on Wall Street and my vision for preserving the spirit of the West are very closely related. I hope you enjoy this volume and find it informative and inspiring.

DAVID R. STOECKLEIN

Ketchum, Idaho

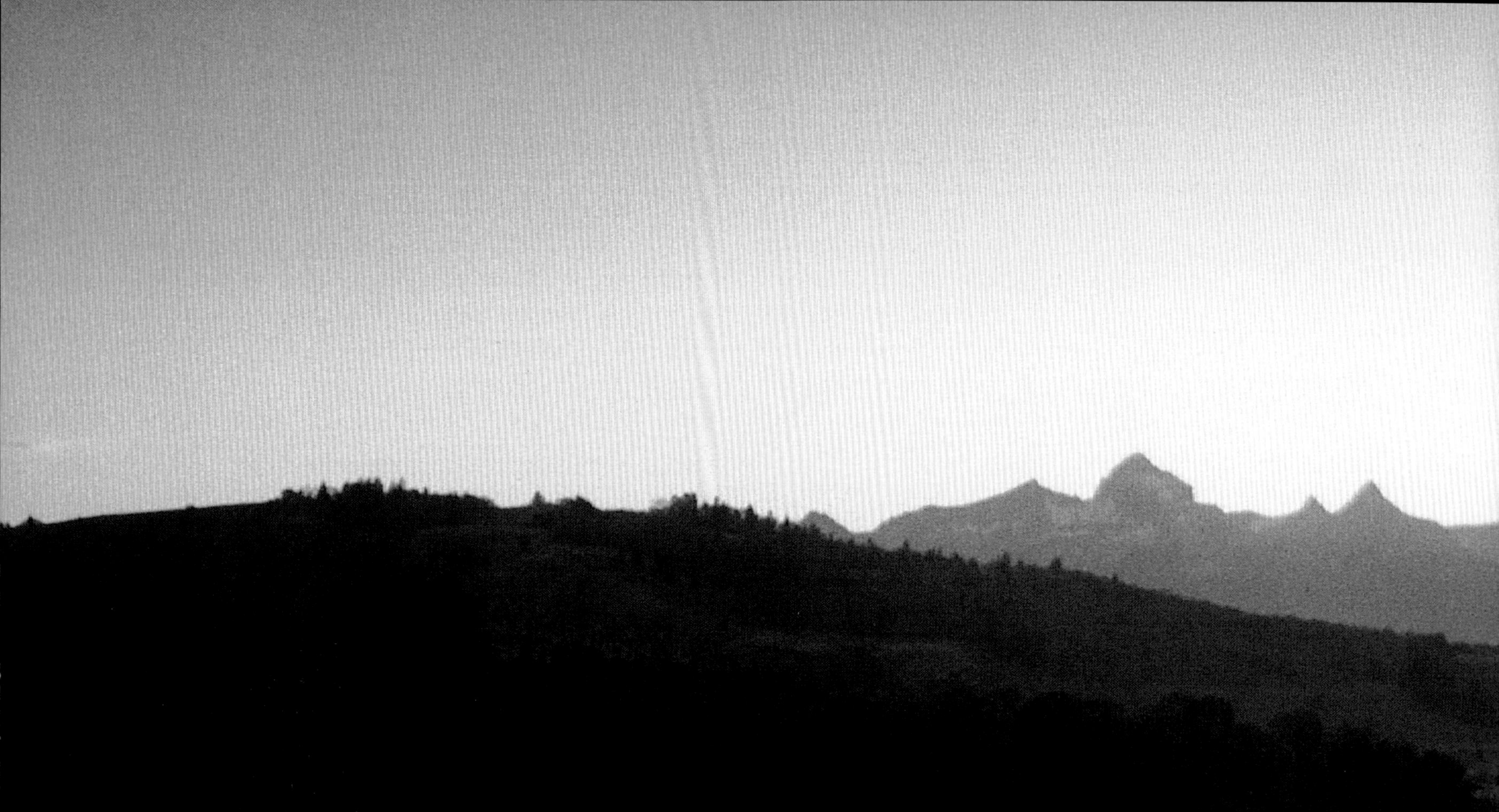

A Personal Journey

Have you ever had a movie change your life? Do you believe that it can even happen? Well, it happened to me. Last year, I saw the movie *Open Range* and somehow, it struck a deep chord in me and got me started down a whole new path in my career.

It was not just the spectacular scenery or the classic showdown between the good guys and the bad guys. It had more to do with the characters played by Robert Duvall and Kevin Costner ~ two cowboys who lived a grueling life in the saddle, yet cared about loyalty and honor above all. It may sound hokey, but that movie took me back to my childhood ~ a time when every boy imagined being the Lone Ranger or Hopalong Cassidy, galloping over the range and rescuing the schoolmarm or the stagecoach driver from peril.

I did not grow up out West, but in Lexington, Kentucky. Still, as I devoured novels by Louis L'Amour and sat watching cowboy heroics at the Saturday matinees, the cattle herds and the Big Sky country never seemed far away. In fact, one of our closest family friends was A.B. Guthrie, Jr., a journalist with the *Lexington Leader* who became one of the country's foremost Western writers. His novel, *The Way West*, won the 1950 Pulitzer Prize, and the screenplay he wrote for *Shane*, the 1953 Western classic starring Alan Ladd, won an Oscar nomination.

I still remember Guthrie's characters, Boone Caudill and Lat Evans, and how much I wanted to possess their kind of quiet strength. As I read about their trials and adventures on the frontier, I longed to be like them ~ to be brave and cool-headed in a crisis and a true-blue friend ~ someone who never hesitated to stand up for what is right. In short, Guthrie's stories made me want to be a better person.

Seeing *Open Range* made all those feelings come flooding back. It reawakened my fascination with the West and its irresistible pull on the imagination. I started reading everything I could find on the subject and have not stopped yet.

The movie also got me thinking anew about the state of our world and the financial industry in which I have worked for over 35 years. Suddenly, things seemed much clearer. Why do we need 20-page contracts when a handshake used to seal a deal? Shouldn't a man's word still be his bond? Didn't we all learn the Golden Rule back in kindergarten? What made us lose sight of the very things that ought to matter the most?

For some time, I have been feeling deep anger and shame at what has happened to our industry. Though the number of blatant wrongdoers may be relatively few, the stain of greed, dishonesty, and impropriety has touched us all. Watching *Open Range*, I felt a tremendous emotional pull ~ a yearning to get back to simpler times when right and wrong were as clear as black and white. I am not saying that

everyone on Wall Street is venal. Making money is what this business is all about, and nobody wants to change that. But it seems that somewhere along the line, our focus on competing and winning at any cost has overrun all other considerations.

In my opinion, something has gone horribly wrong in our business, and our self-preservation depends on fixing it. How can we expect clients to entrust us with their hard-won assets when some of the most venerable, best-known firms in the industry have been tarnished? Wall Street has always operated with a system of self-regulation, but clearly, something in that system is broken.

So what is the answer? For years now, business schools have been teaching courses on ethics. In fact, if you put together all the ethical rules and guidelines adopted by our firms, associations, and regulatory agencies, you would have enough to sink a small battleship.

Can we solve the problem with an even tougher, more specific set of rules that spells out every detail of the way we ought to do business? I don't think so. I do not believe it is possible to devise a set of rules that will lift us out of our quagmire. No one could ever write rules that anticipate and cover every situation. Rules are also difficult to enforce when the stakes are high and wrongdoers think they are smarter than the enforcers. Most importantly, rules alone do not give us a compelling reason to change our ways.

To me, the fundamental problem is that we have confused rules with principles. Rules can always be bent, but principles cannot. So while bureaucratic rules may reinforce the ways we ought to behave, they are no substitute for personal principles. I believe that where human behavior is concerned, any true, lasting change has to come from within. So if we want to encourage better ethical practices throughout the industry, we need something that will touch the deepest part of us ~ something that will make us want to do better and be better than we are.

In short, what we need is not more regulation, but more inspiration. Yet these days, inspiration is not so easy to come by. Think about it: Whom can we look up to as our heroes today? Political leaders, sports figures, corporate CEOs, even people of the church have not remained above greed, corruption, cynicism, and scandal. I feel fortunate to have rediscovered my own heroes and my own source of inspiration. In looking back to one of my earliest passions ~ back to the Old West ~ I have found a way to make more sense of the world and my place in it.

I am not talking about the Old West of Billy the Kid, Wyatt Earp, or Calamity Jane. Truthfully, I am just not interested in gunslingers, Indian fighters, gold prospectors, or dance hall girls. To me, it is the working cowboys who are the true icons of the Old West. They lived the harsh life of the saddle, herding cattle for hundreds of miles across the plains, rivers, and mountains. Far away from the comforts of town and the sheriff's watchful eye, they lived by their own set of rules. Though these rules were unspoken, among cowboys they were known and respected everywhere on the range.

Actually, these so-called "rules of the range" really were not rules at all. They had more to do with character, principles, and values ~ not as you talked about them, but as they were reflected in your actions. It did not matter whether a person was rough around the edges, or hard-looking, or had done some questionable things in the past. What mattered was the kind of person he had become, as revealed by his deeds ~ what kind of man he was when things got rough, or when nobody was looking. The Code of the West was something he held inside, and he knew, in his heart, when he was or was not living up to it.

When you steep yourself in the history of those times and in the time-honored ways of the working cowboy, you realize there is nothing abstract about these values. Cowboys embraced them not as a matter of religious or intellectual belief, but as a matter of day-to-day survival. The work they did was rough, difficult, and dangerous. They had to be able to rely on the integrity and character of the cow-hands that rode with them.

The Code of the West
is based not on myth,
but on the reality of life
on the open range.

LIFE ON THE OPEN RANGE

You cannot understand the cowboy's code without knowing something about his era and the life he led. That story begins with the land, the vast territory that was known as the Great Plains ~ or, as it was labeled on early 19th century maps, "The Great Desert."

It was a hostile, mostly arid environment where temperatures could range from 50 below zero to 120 degrees Fahrenheit in the same spot, depending upon the season and time of day. It is no wonder that few heading out West had any thought of settling in the continent's vast midsection. Few saw it as more than a barren wasteland they had to get across to reach what we know today as Colorado, California, and Oregon.

"You look on, on, on, out into space, out almost

beyond time itself. You see nothing but the rise and

the swell of grass ~ the monotonous, endless prairie!

A stranger traveling on the prairie would get his hopes up,

expecting to see something different on making the next rise.

To him the disappointment and monotony were terrible.

'He's got loneliness,' we would say of such a man."

JOHN NOBLE

Early 20th century Western painter

But this barren land did have one thing ~ plenty of grass to sustain any creature tough enough to withstand the harsh environment. The special breed of cattle known as Texas Longhorns were half-wild descendents of cattle that had been ranched for 300 years in Old Mexico. They were fearsome and mean, reaching up to one ton in weight with wicked horns that could stretch six feet across. But they were perfectly adapted to survival on the open plains and thrived on the prairie grass ~ so much so that when the early Texas settlers arrived, they found hundreds of thousands of cattle running loose throughout the territory and there for the taking. Thus, the great ranches and cattle barons came into being.

It took the railroad to turn the ranches into an industry. In Texas, cattle were so abundant that they were worth no more than $4 per head. But in the country's growing population centers meat was a rare luxury, and that same steer might be worth $40. By 1866, the railroad had reached Missouri and by 1869 it stretched to Kansas. Any rancher who could lead two or three thousand cattle the several hundred miles up to the railheads could make a fortune. That is how the great trail drives came about. Between 1866 and 1885, more than eight million head of cattle were driven up the trails.

At the center of it all was the cowboy. His rugged, simple way of life and the values that go with it loom large in our country's history and mythology. Yet the cowboy's heyday lasted only for a single generation, from the end of the Civil War until 1886, when overgrazing, a summer of drought, and a winter of fierce blizzards wiped out much of the industry. By 1890, barbed wire was closing off the open range and the era of the great trail drives was over. But the cowboy's traditions and his creed have endured, in legend and in practice, right up to the present day.

"Working cowboys are the embodiment of the

true American spirit. They live a rugged, clean life:

a difficult, yet simple life...."

CLINT EASTWOOD

Foreword, *Gathering Remnants: A Tribute to the Working Cowboy* (2000)

LIVING BY THE CODE

By today's standards of social and political correctness, cowboys would hardly be considered models of deportment. They routinely smoked, drank, and cursed, and their table manners were nothing to write home about. They packed guns and sometimes found it necessary to use them. They might not even draw the line at certain kinds of stealing, though it was a hanging offense to steal a man's horse because that could threaten his life.

Yet a cowboy would never dream of disrespecting a lady, taking the last of the water without refilling the bucket, or failing to share his last bit of food with a hungry stranger. The rules of cowboy etiquette were detailed and arcane. To know them, you had to be intimately familiar with life on the range. They covered any number of situations ~ when you could begin to eat, when you could wear your hat indoors, what to do if you came across a downed fence, where to leave your gun when you entered someone's house.

Cowboy ethics, on the other hand, were far simpler. Knowing right from wrong, following the Golden Rule, and being willing to work hard would take you a long way.

Was there any more to it than that? Was there really such a thing as a Code of the West? Having pored over stacks of books on the subject over the past year, I can tell you that yes, there really was a code that working cowboys valued and lived by. It was the product of a unique place and time. Before the American West was

settled and barbed wire closed off the plains, there was no framework of law. For the cowboy, the Code was the one civilizing influence that could be relied upon.

The interesting thing is that no one can say with authority exactly what the Code of the West was. It was not carved in stone; in fact, it was not even written down on paper. Yet, while not every cowboy always abided by the Code, every cowboy knew what it was. Based upon everything I have learned in my research, I believe I know too.

What follows is my own list of the ten principles that capture the essence of the Code of the West. They are true to the spirit of the open range, yet still have meaning for us today.

The CODE of the WEST

1   Live Each Day with Courage

2   Take Pride in Your Work

3   Always Finish What You Start

4   Do What Has to Be Done

5   Be Tough, But Fair

6   When You Make a Promise, Keep It

7   Ride for the Brand

8   Talk Less and Say More

9   Remember That Some Things Aren't For Sale

10 Know Where to Draw the Line

spirit

respect

honor

perseverance

LIVE EACH DAY
WITH COURAGE

"A man wanting in courage would be as much out of place in a cow-camp

as a fish on dry land. Indeed the life he is daily compelled to lead

calls for the existence of the highest degree of cool calculating courage."

Texas Livestock Journal (1882)

There is an old saying that "a cowboy's a man with guts and a horse." No one lacking in bravery could last very long on the range. Trailing beeves, as the cowboys called it, was dangerous enough on a good day. Cowboys encountered stampedes, quicksand, torrential rivers, clouds of alkaline dust that burned the lungs, hostile Indians, and other life-threatening dangers.

Yet cowboys cheerfully braved all these perils so they could sleep under the stars and earn seventy-five or eighty cents a day. Even so, their demonstrations of grit earned them no special recognition or praise from the boss, or even from their fellow cowboys. The virtues of fortitude and courage were part of the cowboy's stock-in-trade ~ something to be remarked upon only in their absence. Cowards were not to be tolerated, because one coward could endanger the whole group.

Real courage is being scared to death

and saddling up anyway.

If you suspect that the courageous cowboy is only a Hollywood myth, read the words of John R. Erickson, a fine Western writer who has also lived the cowboy life, from his book, *Some Babies Grow Up To Be Cowboys* (1999).

"The heroism of the working cowboy isn't a joke...

it isn't something that has been cooked up by an advertising agency,

and it isn't something that cheap minds will ever understand.

Cowboys are heroic because they exercise human courage

on a daily basis. They live with danger. They take chances.

They sweat, they bleed, they burn in the summer and freeze

in the winter. They find out how much a mere human can do,

and then they do a little more. They reach beyond themselves."

This is not to say that cowboys never knew fear ~ only that they were able to put their fear aside when there was work to be done.

There is more to courage than jumping into a river to save someone's life. It is also being willing to speak up and say that something isn't right ~ even if that means going up against partners, colleagues, or superiors.

TAKE PRIDE
IN YOUR WORK

The cowboy is often portrayed as being unlettered and unskilled ~ a common laborer in spurs. In the cowboy's own mind, he was no mere work hand, but a cavalier ~ a knight of the plains sitting tall in the saddle. The cowboy's pride grew from his riding and roping skills, his indifference to danger and deprivation, and his capacity for hard work.

It is true that cowboys disdained work they could not do from horseback. They might rather ride twenty miles in a howling blizzard than dig postholes. But if there was a job that needed doing, no matter how humble, a cowboy was obliged to do it, and do it the best he could.

A poem by Red Steagall, the Official Cowboy Poet of Texas, beautifully evokes this principle. Titled *The Fence That Me and Shorty Built,* it is the tale of an old cowpoke who watches a young hire shirking a mundane job he resents. The old hand remembers how years earlier, he had felt the same way until Shorty, a wiser and more experienced hand, set him straight. These are the stanzas that get to the heart of it:

Son, I ain't much on schoolin',

Didn't get too far with that.

But there's a lot of learnin'

Hidden underneath this hat.

I got it all the hard way,

Every bump and bruise and fall.

Now some of it was easy,

But then most weren't fun a'tall.

But one thing that I always got

From every job I've done,

Is do the best I can each day

And try to make it fun.

I know that bustin' through them rocks

Ain't what you like to do.

By gettin' mad you've made it tough

On me and all the crew.

Now you hired on to cowboy

And you think you've got the stuff.

You told him you're a good hand

And the boss has called your bluff.

So how's that gonna make you look

When he comes ridin' through,

And he asks me who dug the holes

And I say it was you.

Now we could let it go like this

And take the easy route.

But doin' things the easy way

Ain't what it's all about.

The boss expects a job well done,

From every man he's hired.

He'll let you slide by once or twice,

Then one day you'll get fired.

If you're not proud of what you do,

You won't amount to much.

You'll bounce around from job to job

Just slightly out of touch.

Come mornin' let's re-dig those holes

And get that fence in line.

And you and I will save two jobs,

Those bein' yours and mine.

And someday you'll come ridin' through

And look across this land,

And see a fence that's laid out straight

And know you had a hand,

In something that's withstood the years.

Then proud and free from guilt,

You'll smile and say, "Boys, that's

The fence that me and Shorty built."

Excerpt from the book *The Fence That Me and Shorty Built* with permission from Red Steagall

Cowboying doesn't build character.

It reveals it.

What your teacher told you back in first grade still holds true: Anything worth doing is worth doing well.

ALWAYS FINISH
WHAT YOU START

"No cowboy ever quit while his life was hardest

and his duties were most exacting."

J. FRANK DOBIE, *A Vaquero of the Brush Country* (1929)

Cowboys hated quitters. They hated whining and complaining almost as much, because those things had the stench of quitting. On a trail drive, it was when things got roughest that every hand was expected to give his all.

There is a great scene in Howard Hawks's classic Western film, *Red River*, that perfectly captures the steeliness of cowboy resolve. John Wayne plays Thomas Dunson, who in 1851 arrives in Texas with nothing but big dreams and a quick draw. Fourteen years later, he has built a cattle empire only to face financial ruin in the economic collapse of Texas following the Civil War. His only hope is to drive his cattle a thousand miles to Missouri, where they will be worth a small fortune. Others have attempted the journey, but nobody has made it yet.

Let's face it ~ these last few years

haven't been the easiest of times.

But on days when things seem

especially rough, I think about

what it must have been like

on the open range in the middle

of a blizzard, and I tell myself,

"Cowboy up."

The night before setting out, Dunson lets his cowhands know what they are up against. If the herd makes ten miles a day, they will be doing well, and they are sure to encounter Indians, dry wells, and foul weather, he warns. Once they get to Missouri, they will have to deal with "border gangs" intent on killing as many men and stealing as many cattle as they can. "Nobody has to come along," Dunson tells his men. "We'll still have a job for you when we get back." Then, raising his voice, he adds:

> *"But remember this: Every man who signs*
> *on for the drive agrees to finish it.*
> *There'll be no quitting along the way ~*
> *not by me, not by you."*

It is impossible to watch John Wayne deliver those lines and not say to yourself, "If I were one of those cowboys, I would make it to Missouri, or die trying."

keep riding.

Do What Has To Be Done

"Whenever there is [trouble], we'll depend on ourselves.
We'll take care of it ~ when it comes, not after it's too late."

WILL JAMES, *The American Cowboy* (1942)

The classic Western hero is the man who stands up for what is right ~ who rectifies injustice wherever he sees it and exacts retribution when it is due. That is what the Code of the West demanded. To the cowboy, it was a matter of honor to do the right thing even ~ and especially ~ when the odds were fearsomely stacked against him. Out on the range, the true test of a man's honor was how much he would risk to keep it intact. Take, for example, the movie *High Noon*, in which Gary Cooper, as Sheriff Will Kane, is left alone to defend the town against a murderous band of outlaws. In answer to the pleadings of his Quaker wife, Kane simply says, "I've got to, that's the whole thing."

In the classic Western films such as *High Noon*, *The Unforgiven*, and more recently, *Open Range*, the plot goes beyond the simple clash of good and evil. Strong as

the hero may be, he always faces an enemy who is equally formidable, if not more so. He faces the prospect that his stand will cost him dearly ~ maybe even cost him his life. And he faces the ultimate questions: What will I do in the moment of truth? Will I have the courage to stand up for what is right?

In Kevin Costner's *Open Range*, the cowboy heroes are Boss Spearman, a tough old cattle drover who has endeavored to steer clear of bloodshed, and his hand Charley Waite, who has clearly done some killing in his time. While resting their herd, they run up against Baxter, a despotic rancher who rules the nearby town and hates "free grazers" like Boss and Charley. Baxter's men rough up their friend, Mose, and the bullying rancher lets them know he means to kill them all and scatter their herd if they do not quit his domain.

"You reckon them cows are worth getting killed over?" Charley asks Boss when he vows to protect the herd. "The cows is one thing," says Boss. "But one man telling another where he can go in this country is something else." After Baxter's thugs kill Mose, leave another hand for dead, and even shoot the dog, there is no question

The true test of a man's honor was

what Boss and Charley must do. Girded for a showdown, they find the townspeople sympathetic, but too cowed to join the fight. "I didn't raise my boys to see them killed," says one business owner. "You may not know it," Charley replies, "but there's things that gnaw at a man worse than dying."

Knowing that all hell is about to break loose, Charley, who has faced the barrel of a gun more than once, hatches a desperate plan to take down the eight men gunning for them. "You've got it all worked out," Boss says approvingly. "Yeah," says Charley, "everything except the part where we don't get killed."

While smoking a last Cuban cigar, they reflect on what they will miss if they do not succeed ~ the dream of an easier life, in Boss's case, and a newfound chance at happiness with Sue Barlow in Charley's. While we know it would not do for the bad guys to win in the end, the outcome of the gunfight really is not the point. What matters is that Boss and Charley could have rounded up their cattle and left trouble behind. But they didn't.

It's not always easy

to do the right thing.

But nobody said it would be.

how much he would risk to keep it intact.

BE TOUGH,
BUT FAIR

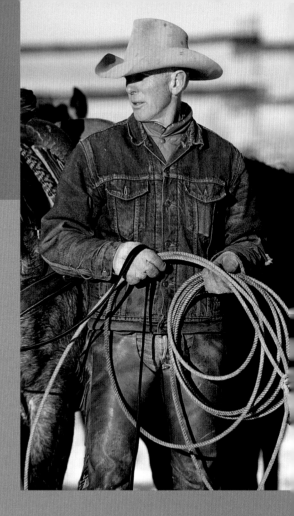

"I won't be wronged, I won't be insulted, and I won't be laid a hand on.
I don't do these things to other people and I require the same from them."

JOHN WAYNE in his last film, *The Shootist* (1976)

Everyone knows that cowboys of the Old West were as tough as nails. Living in wide-open spaces far beyond the reach of authority, they had to be. They often carried guns for protection against Indians, wild beasts, and marauders. They dealt swiftly with rustlers and horse thieves. And their pride made them notably intolerant of insults to them, their outfit, or their way of life.

But our popular image of the cowboy overlooks the way his toughness was tempered by other elements of his Code ~ the ones demanding fairness in all dealings. In practice, the notion of fair play was deeply ingrained in every facet of prairie life. Cowboys on the open range felt honor-bound to give those they encountered a "square deal," as Teddy Roosevelt called it, and they depended on others to treat them the same way. The Code was the framework for a symbiotic social order that raised the odds of survival in a tough business and a harsh land.

For example, extending open hospitality to anyone who needed it was an ironclad rule. A traveler had the right to enter any ranch house at any time of day or night, even if the occupants were away, to avail himself of food and shelter. He was even free to take those supplies required for the next leg of his journey. While he was not expected to pay for the ranch owner's hospitality, the Code called for him to make his recompense to another hungry stranger somewhere down the line.

There is a famous story of a greedy rancher who fed two cowboys who were down on their luck, but then demanded that they pay for their dinner. This breach so outraged the hands that they branded one of his calves with giant letters spelling out "MEALS ~ 50 cents." Along the same vein, if a cow bearing a neighbor's brand wandered into a rancher's herd, he was not expected to return the stray, as that could mean a journey of fifty miles or more. He was free to sell the animal along with his own herd. But he was also obligated to pay his neighbor the price he received for the cow plus any calves she may have dropped. Ranchers everywhere abided by this rule, as their cattle were equally prone to wander across the unfenced range.

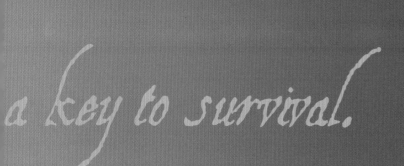

a key to survival.

Under the cattle country definition of fair play, a deal was a deal, a handshake was as good as a written contract, and there was no such thing as reneging on a debt. As the legendary cattleman Oliver Loving was lying on his deathbed, his mind was troubled by some debts he had incurred. His partner, Charles Goodnight, paid tribute to his friend's deep sense of honor by keeping their partnership in force until his debts could be paid in full.

Cowboys of the Old West were workers, not gunslingers, and they did not go looking for trouble. But when trouble found them, the rules were unequivocal. If someone was killed in a fair fight, that was not murder, it was an incident. On the other hand, shooting an unarmed or fleeing man ~ even if he was a sworn enemy ~ was strictly forbidden, and transgressors were quickly brought to frontier justice.

On the open range, cowboys shared a way of life that was as difficult and tenuous as it was rewarding. So they had a natural self-interest in honoring the Code's insistence on fair play. For them, the Golden Rule was not something learned in Sunday school. The principle of "do unto others what you would have them do unto you" was nothing more and nothing less than a key to survival.

WHEN YOU MAKE A PROMISE, KEEP IT

When it came to keeping his word, a cowboy's allegiance to principle was absolute. He was bound to fulfill his promise, no matter what. This theme is vividly rendered in *Lonesome Dove*, Larry McMurtry's Pulitzer Prize-winning book. It is arguably the Great American Novel, and the television version starring Robert Duvall and Tommy Lee Jones ranks as one of the best Westerns ever made. As the saga of the two former Texas Rangers draws to a close, Augustus McRae and Woodrow Call have driven their herd all the way to Montana, where they intend to start a ranch. Gus and his hand, Pea Eye, are scouting for a site when they are attacked by Indians and Gus takes two arrows in the leg. Worse still, the Indians kill their horses.

Surrounded, the two dig in for the night next to a riverbank, the only cover they can find. By morning Gus is feverish. After all the travails he has endured, Gus's luck has run out. Pea Eye goes for help, losing his clothes at the first river crossing, and walking naked for three days until he reaches the trail drive's encampment.

By the time Call catches up with his partner, Gus has been rescued and one leg has been amputated. But the other leg is now gangrenous; clearly, the end is near.

A man is only as good as his word.

Gus tells Call he wants a favor: He wants to be buried back in Texas, in an orchard where he had some happy times. Call thinks his friend is delirious. "You want me to haul you to Texas?" he exclaims. "We just got to Montana." "I got nothing against wintering in Montana," Gus replies. "Just pack me in salt or charcoal or what you will. I'll keep well enough and you can make the trip in the spring." Pointing out that Gus will never know if he keeps his promise, Call relents, saying "I reckon I'll do it, since you've asked."

Spring comes and Call gets ready to haul Gus's preserved remains back to Texas, telling his hands he will be back in a year. From the day of Gus's death, everyone has told Call his friend was drunk or out of his mind to ask such a favor. Call agrees the whole thing is foolish but, as he says, "a promise is a promise."

The 3,000-mile journey does not go smoothly, and Call makes the last leg dragging the coffin behind his horse on a makeshift travois. As he digs Gus's grave with a hand shovel, he is weak and his water has run out. The digging takes all day and when he is done, Call feels he is about ready to be buried himself. "There," he mutters under his breath. "This will teach me to be more careful about what I promise."

If you think about it,

investors only need

two things from Wall Street:

~ someone they can trust

~ someone they can count on.

49

Ride For The Brand

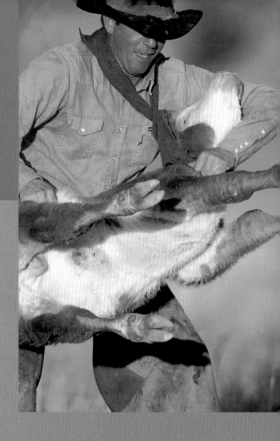

"They were intensely loyal to the outfit

they were working for and would fight to the death for it.

They would follow their wagon boss through hell and never complain."

"TEDDY BLUE" ABBOTT, *We Pointed Them North: Recollections of a Cowpuncher* (1939)

This is one cowboy principle that is often misunderstood. It is true that once a cowboy tossed his bedroll into an outfit's wagon, he was obliged to put its needs ahead of his own. Any personal hardships or complaints were to be swallowed the same way he swallowed his coffee. His loyalty came through in his unstinting hard work, his cheerfulness, and his fervent defense of the outfit against any harm or slur.

But riding for the brand did not mean giving the boss blind, unquestioning allegiance. Cowpunchers were not cut out to toady to someone just because he counted out their pay at the end of the month. As Teddy Roosevelt observed, "Cowboys call no man master."

The cowboy's greatest devotion was to his calling and his way of life. So his loyalties naturally centered upon those who valued his traditions and counted upon him to uphold them. In short, the cowboy gave allegiance and respect where they were deserved and returned.

One of Red Steagall's best-known poems eloquently speaks to these nuances. Titled *Ride for the Brand*, it tells of the Waggoner Ranch and a leathery, hard-bitten old cowpoke named Jake who is schooling "the new kid" in the unwritten laws of the range. This passage puts the idea of loyalty to the boss in context:

> Son, a man's brand is his own special mark,
> It says "This is mine. Leave it alone."
> You hire out to a man, you ride for his brand
> And protect it like it was your own.
>
> He said, Mister Waggoner come out here in 1903,
> This country was sagebrush, mesquite trees and sand.
> He carved him this ranch out of blood, sweat and guts,
> So be proud that you ride for his brand.

If you work in the investment industry, make no mistake about where your loyalties should lie: The client comes first ~ not when it's convenient, not when you feel like it, but always!

Excerpt from the book *Ride for the Brand* with permission from Red Steagall

his calling and his way of life.

TALK LESS
AND SAY MORE

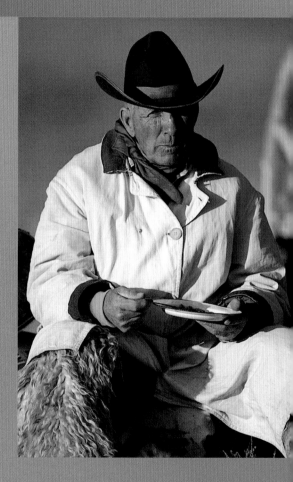

In the old Saturday matinees, the cowboy was always a man of few words ~ the strong, silent type. In real life, too, cowboys were not exactly what you would call garrulous. In the cowboy's mind, "the bigger the mouth, the better it looks shut." That is why he ranked lawyers and other windbags not much higher than cattle rustlers. Who can forget the sight of Clint Eastwood spitting tobacco juice on the fast-talking peddler's white spats in *The Outlaw Josey Wales*?

Maybe it was the isolation, or the stark contrast between flat earth and blue sky, or the grandeur of nature overwhelming the puniness of small talk. For whatever reason, cowboys avoided empty verbiage. They were doers, not talkers. And when they did talk they got straight to the point. When a trail boss said of a cowboy, "He's a good hand," that was the highest praise he could bestow. Likewise, an admiring hand might say of his employer, "That boss...he sure can cowboy."

The cowboy's preference for clipped commentary became part of his trademark ~ something that marked him as surely as his hat and pointed boots. But it would be a mistake to think that cowboys were unexpressive. A better description would be

When there's nothing more to say,

don't be saying it.

I've learned over the years that when it comes to communicating with clients, the most important rule is keep it simple...keep it true.

"sententious," meaning terse or pithy in expression. Cowboys had an undeniable gift for speaking in concise, often-colorful phrases and word-pictures that distilled thoughts down to their essence.

As cowboy chronicler Ramon F. Adams put it, they "laid firm hands on language and squeezed the juice right out of it." This gift for phrasemaking is one reason why a strong tradition of cowboy poetry still flourishes today. Make no mistake: Cowboy talk could be crude and laced with profanity. But even the coarsest expressions were usually delivered with a grin, and in between the cuss-words and barnyard imagery, cowboys had a way of making things both simple and profound.

Being mostly uneducated, cowboys were not bound by the rules of grammar or polite discourse. Their words came straight from their experience of life, which gave them a powerful originality and directness. Cowboys said what they meant. They also understood that when words are scarce, the ones you do say become all the more important.

Remember That Some Things Aren't For Sale

One of the most underrated classic Western films is *Monte Walsh*, the Turner Network Television remake recently released on DVD. Tom Selleck was born to play the role of a turn-of-the-century Wyoming cowboy who is watching his way of life disappear. The combination of deadly winters and "progress" has doomed the small ranchers, and what herds remain are being taken over by large, faceless corporations. Monte is fast becoming an anachronism, and he knows it.

As work and money dwindle, Monte is driven to consider the unthinkable. He resigns himself to looking for a job in town ~ one that might even pay enough to let him settle down and marry a local saloon girl, the one woman he is comfortable with. One day, while breaking a wild horse and nearly wrecking half the town in the process, Monte catches the eye of the proprietor of a traveling Wild West show. Envisioning Monte as his next star attraction, the showman offers him a job playing a "real cowboy" for the princely sum of $15 a week ~ more money than he could hope to earn anywhere else.

Our industry is known for being full of smart people. But think about it: How smart can we be if we don't value our reputations above all else?

58

To the cowboy, the best things

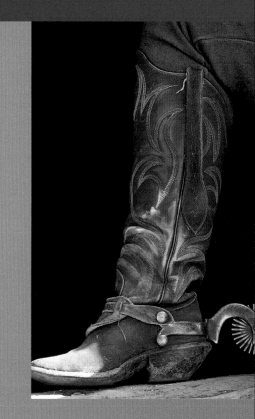

Monte reluctantly accepts, but the moment of truth comes when he puts on the garish fringed costume and ridiculous hat he has been given and looks in the mirror. Disgusted by what he has been reduced to, Monte rebels. "I ain't spittin' on my whole life," he says, taking off the hat and handing it to the stunned promoter. With this simple gesture Monte throws away his one chance for a new start, but for him, there really is no choice. No amount of money is enough to make him cheapen and dishonor the way of life he has chosen.

The movie does not have a particularly happy ending. Monte's best friend is murdered and his would-be fiancée dies of pneumonia. We even see him stepping his horse aside from the path of a horseless carriage driven by the pompous twit who took his job away. But Monte is still in the saddle and in the last frames of the movie, as the primitive automobile is mired in the mud, he jumps his horse right over it and rides off into the sunset. Though he cannot hold back the future, he will hold on to his dignity.

Know Where
To Draw the Line

Just because something isn't illegal doesn't mean it's right.

"Good fences make good neighbors," wrote the New England poet, Robert Frost. But out West, people looked at things differently. On the open range, the boundaries people needed to get along were set by shared standards of right and wrong. Those boundaries were as good as fences because everyone knew where they were.

Hud is a story about drawing clear lines between right and wrong in an era when that idea seemed hopelessly out of fashion. With Paul Newman in the title role, the 1963 film tells of the conflict between Homer Bannon, an elderly cattle rancher who stubbornly holds onto his principles, and his son Hud, who cares about nothing but himself.

The rancor between father and son flares up when Homer finds a heifer dead for no apparent cause. Over Hud's angry protests, Homer calls in a government vet, who warns the Bannons to expect the worst. If the cow died from foot-and-mouth disease as he suspects, the entire herd will have to be destroyed.

To Hud, this means losing the inheritance he is counting on to support his hard-drinking, devil-may-care lifestyle. He spends far more time in his pink '57 Cadillac than tending cattle. But to Homer it is a devastating blow. His herd is all he has to show for a lifetime of hard work.

Hud offers him an easy way out: He will get on the phone and sell the cattle the next day, before the tests can confirm the disease. But Homer will not even discuss it; he would never consider passing diseased cattle on to his neighbors. When Hud suggests selling them out of state, Homer can scarcely believe his ears. "What?" he says. "And take a chance on starting an epidemic in the entire country?"

At this, Hud explodes. "This whole country is run on epidemics; where you been?" he sneers, ticking off the litany of wrongdoing he sees all around ~ "price fixing, crooked TV shows, income tax finagling, souped-up expense accounts. How many honest men d'you know?" he demands.

Homer will not be swayed, though he knows his honesty carries a heavy price. He must watch as the entire herd he has painstakingly bred and crossbred is prodded into pits, shot, and buried by bulldozers.

As if that were not enough, he must destroy the two rare Texas Longhorns he has raised himself. Among the last of their breed, they are Homer's reminder of a vanishing way of life. "Let's turn 'em loose," suggests Lon, Hud's young nephew, who wants to spare his grandfather this ultimate pain. "No, that wouldn't be the thing to do," the old man replies. "They've got to go along with the rest."

Homer knows it does not require a big fall from grace for men to lose their integrity. It most often happens by degrees, as corners are cut and minor misdeeds rationalized, each small step leading to another. And so the world changes, little by little, except for those who stay stubbornly true to their own beliefs.

Knowing Lon is half-repelled, half-attracted by Hud's free-wheeling ways, Homer tells him he must make up his own mind as to what is right and what is wrong. While history tells us why the Cowboy's Code fit the days of the open range, modern-day tales in films such as *Hud* tell us why the Code of the West is timeless.

and nothing in between.

A Call to Action

HOW COWBOY ETHICS CAN CHANGE OUR INDUSTRY

I have described the Cowboy's Code as "ten timeless principles to live by," because that is exactly what they are. I believe the Code can offer meaningful inspiration and guidance to anyone.

The Code of the West is especially relevant to Wall Street because, like our industry, cowboys operated with a system of self-regulation. Either you lived up to the Code or you were shunned. And like us, cowboys had compelling practical reasons to embrace their Code. As a matter of survival, they needed to know they could depend on the integrity and character of those who rode with them. In the same way, our clients must be able to trust us to handle their assets; our business survival depends on it.

The challenge we face as an industry is figuring out how we can redeem our reputations and earn back investors' trust. One thing I know is that we cannot do it with words. No matter how eloquent or high-flown, words can only ring hollow in investors' ears. The only way we can do it is with our actions ~ actions that reflect the character, principles, and values at our core.

This is the take-home lesson from Cowboy Ethics: Everyone needs a code ~ a creed to live by.

John Wayne said that ~ and so did William Donaldson, chairman of the Securities and Exchange Commission, when he spoke to the National Association of Securities Dealers in May of 2004. In essence, he told the NASD that while the SEC is vigorously pursuing enforcement actions against wrongdoers and promulgating a host of new ethical rules, the SEC cannot do the whole job alone.

Quoting Donaldson, "...our rules alone won't be enough. Our rules never have been enough, are not enough today, and never will be enough. What's really needed is a change in mindset ~ one that fosters not only a 'culture of compliance' but also a company-wide environment that fosters ethical behavior and decision-making."

What does a "culture of compliance" mean? In the SEC Chairman's own words, it means instilling "a company-wide commitment to do the right thing, this time and every time" so that ethical behavior becomes "the core of the company's essential DNA" and is "shared by every employee." It means a firm's leaders should have the "courage and commitment" to question whether a particular practice is truly ethical or truly in the best interests of clients and customers, no matter what the lawyers say. It means that "customers always come before the balance sheet and not the other way around."

The SEC is doing its part by taking enforcement actions against the "bad guys" who compromise the integrity of our entire industry. The rest of the job is up to the ninety percent of us who want to do the right thing. We are the ones who need to set the tone by embracing a meaningful set of corporate values and living by them each and every day.

If we fail to act, if we fail to create a culture that fosters doing the right thing, we risk losing the privilege of self-regulation. Think about it: Do we really want the lawyers to come in and run our businesses? We who count ourselves among the "good guys" cannot just sit by silently and let that happen. If we do, it will be our fault as much as the fault of those who cheated, lied, and covered up. That day will soon be here if we don't act, and act now.

I do not deny that "instilling corporate values" sounds like a mushy, amorphous task ~ one that could be awfully tough to get your arms around. But we can break it down into a to-do list that we can all start working on right away. As a start, here are my suggestions:

First, every firm registered with the SEC should appoint a Director of Corporate Values who is charged with overseeing ethical principles and practices concerning every activity of the firm. I am not talking about someone who is off in a corner dusting off mission statements and churning out yet another batch of compliance manuals. I am talking about a senior-level individual with the stature to represent the firm's commitment to living by a code. While the Chief Compliance Officer's job is to meet the letter of the law, the job of the Director of Corporate Values would be to fulfill the spirit of the law. If you are not sure whom to tap for the job, pick the person who makes everyone stand a little straighter when he or she walks into the room.

Secondly, adopt a code and apply this set of principles to every decision of consequence. This code does not have to be emblazoned on a brass plate set in mahogany; what matters is that you live by the code each day. I have to admit that at my own firm, a growing hedge fund of funds advisor named Austin Capital Management, my partners were initially skeptical about embracing the Cowboy Code, wondering if it was really more than just a gimmick. Then we began consciously to apply Cowboy Ethics to our daily business practices.

The results were startling. In most cases, the "right thing" to do was surprisingly clear. When the issue was particularly thorny, difficult, or personal, our discussions would quickly get right to the heart of the matter: What is fair? Where do we want to draw the line? What are we unwilling to compromise? Putting it in those terms helped give us the courage and resolve to make difficult choices and do what had to be done. My firm has now adopted the ten cowboy principles as the centerpiece of our ethical code, and I urge you to do the same.

Third, we can make sure that integrity and character are key factors in every hiring and partnering decision. Our industry is a magnet for amazingly bright, talented people, but we need to look beyond the SAT scores and the résumés to the inner core of those we choose to work for us and for our clients. At my own firm, we see brainpower and hard work as a given ~ the baseline requirement. As we evaluate candidates, we put personal integrity and character at the very top of the list.

There are many other things that firms can do: Have periodic meetings where colleagues discuss ethical issues they have faced. Build ethical considerations into procedural guidelines. Have the CEO or Managing Partner address all employees on the importance of corporate values. Tell our clients the high expectations they should have of us, and put it in writing ~ not in dense, cover-your-rear-end lega-lese, but in plain, straightforward language.

We also need organizations such as the Investment Management Consultants Association to get out in front on this issue and lead at the industry level. I am singling out IMCA® not because I helped found the group, but because over its 19-year history, IMCA has demonstrated its commitment to raising the level of

professionalism in the industry. But there is still work to be done, and I believe that IMCA has the potential to step up and act as the conscience of the industry.

With all the talent and energy in IMCA and perhaps other organizations, we can surely find some fresh, practical ways to help investment firms create the culture of doing right. Through these industry groups, firms can also work together instead of separately reinventing the wheel. There is a time to compete and a time to cooperate ~ and we need to recognize that we are all in this together.

I believe the only way we can truly transform our industry is from the inside out. Ultimately, that means leadership starts with the individual. We do not have to sit back and wait passively for our firms and organizations to step forward; we all have the potential to lead by example. We can each embrace our own code, and reflect it in the things we do each day. And we can speak out when we see things our partners, colleagues, and firms should be doing differently.

Speaking for myself, I can tell you that since starting this project, I think about things on a whole different level. I have taken the Cowboy Code to heart, and I am making a conscious effort to live by it each day. My life has changed as a result, and I hope the difference comes through in my business and personal relationships. Cowboy Ethics has changed my life and, I believe, has the potential to change the industry from the inside out.

You may feel that the Cowboy's Code does not fit our times, and it is true that few of us will ever be called to test our courage against perils anything like a raging blizzard or a runaway herd of cattle. But we can have the courage to give clients an honest account of bad news, or to confront a business practice that does not put the client first. Every time we make a decision, we can ask ourselves "Is it right? Is it fair?" We can decide that our honor and our reputations are not for sale. At a time when heroes are in short supply...

We can all be heroes in our own lives.

ACKNOWLEDGEMENTS

PHOTOGRAPHER

DAVID STOECKLEIN STOECKLEIN PHOTOGRAPHY & PUBLISHING

From the first moment I saw David's images of the West, I was stunned at how perfectly they capture the cowboy spirit ~ the nobility of the men, their love of their way of life, and the majesty of their surroundings. His artistry and his dedication to "the cowboy way" have been an inspiration. I am honored to have his work appear with mine.

COLLABORATING WRITER

BRIGITTE LEBLANC LEBLANC & COMPANY

Over the past decade, Brigitte and I have worked hand-in-hand on virtually everything I've put into print. Besides serving as wordsmith and translator for my concepts, she helps me shape the content flow and framework. I'm proud of all the things we've done together, but this project will always be closest to my heart.

ART DIRECTOR | DESIGNER

NITA ALVAREZ THE ALVAREZ GROUP INC.

Nita has been the graphic designer for all of my publication and presentation projects since 1986. As a Texas native, she was also the perfect muse and content advisor for this project. Although based in Los Angeles now, she's still got that cowgirl spirit. Her dad, Delmar, was a genuine cowboy in his youth and I think that gave her a special feeling for the words and images that comes through in the finished product.

EDITOR

CARRIE LIGHTNER *Managing Editor & Producer* STOECKLEIN PHOTOGRAPHY & PUBLISHING

There is a real art to editing, and Carrie is a master of it. Her handling of the text was light, but firm, and everything she touched was better for it.

LITHOGRAPHER

STAN CARTER APPLE GRAPHICS

Through many years and nearly as many printing projects, I have learned to count on Stan's unwavering dedication and attention to detail. Our team is fortunate to have had Stan in charge of bringing our project to life on the printed page.

PHOTO RESEARCHER

KENDRA KINGHORN *Stock Photography Manager* STOECKLEIN PHOTOGRAPHY & PUBLISHING

As the overseer of David Stoecklein's 10,000-image archive, Kendra helped us immeasurably in finding the right match between photographs and text.

MY INSPIRATION

In the course of this project I pored over dozens of books on cowboys and the West ~ well over a hundred in all. I read many authors who were knowledgeable and interesting, but no one penetrates more deeply into the core of the cowboy's being than Western author and real-life cowboy, **JOHN ERICKSON**. Every time I asked myself, "Just what is it that makes cowboys so special?," I could pick up one of his books and find an answer ringing with truth and eloquence.

MY PARTNERS AND COLLEAGUES

I could never ask for better partners than **CHUCK RILEY** and **BRENT MARTIN**. Throughout this year-long project, they were totally supportive and encouraging. All I can say is, "Pards, you'll do to ride the river with." I also want to thank **KENDALL COURTNEY** and **WILL GRAY** at Austin Capital Management. "You two can watch my back anytime."

THE IMCA BOARD AND STAFF

I will be forever indebted to **EVELYN BRUST,** who recently retired as Executive Director of the Investment Management Consultants Association, and to the IMCA Board. Not only did they endorse the concept of Cowboy Ethics, they gave me the keynote address at The IMCA 2004 Fall Money Management Exposition as my platform. IMCA gave me the opportunity to air my ideas, and this book was the direct result. I would also like to recognize **NORM NABHAN**, President, and **LEE ZIMMERMAN**, Executive Director, for their leadership and vision.

MY WIFE

STANYA has been the inspiration for everything good I've done in my life. I would never have been able to take on this project, much less finish it, were it not for her understanding and tolerance. As she watched me pour heart and soul into this book, she not only indulged my passion, but fueled it, providing insights that always helped me take my thinking to a higher level. "Stanya, I cannot imagine riding into the sunset with anyone but you."